THE NOVEL IN ENGLISH
AN INTRODUCTION

Macmillan International College Edition

Titles of related interest:

General Editor: Professor A. N. Jeffares, University of Stirling

G. J. Watson: *Drama: An Introduction*
Charles Barber: *Poetry in English: An Introduction*
Richard Taylor: *Understanding the Elements of Literature*
M. M. Badawi: *Background to Shakespeare*
Bruce King: *The New English Literatures*
Bruce King: *West Indian Literature*
S. H. Burton and C. J. H. Chacksfield: *African Poetry in English*

THE NOVEL IN ENGLISH

AN INTRODUCTION

Ian Milligan

M

First published 1983 by
THE MACMILLAN PRESS LTD
London and Basingstoke
Companies and representatives throughout the world

Typeset by Thames Typesetting,
Abingdon, Oxon

Printed in Hong Kong

ISBN 0 333 32438 2
ISBN 0 333 32439 0 Pbk

Contents

Foreword

There are so many novels, and they are so varied in subject, style and achievement. They bear witness to the curiosity of mankind about itself, they show us how writers see men and women in their societies, and they often demonstrate men and women coming to terms with society in the process of growing up, of learning, of making crucial judgements, of taking decisions, either carrying out actions themselves or reacting to the thoughts, the emotions, the behaviour of others. And behind all this analysis and action, this dialogue and description, this creation which reaches into realism or the infinities of imagination, or mingles these extremes, there is, almost inevitably, the human desire to tell a story, a story about people. Once upon a time . . . He spoke to her, and she replied to him . . . The door opened and the golden light irradiated the room where . . .

The European novel, the English novel, the American novel have different nuances, but their general achievement has been the creation of a world, a fictional world where fact and fancy have intermingled, a populous world in which we find the living characters the novelists have created: men and women who have a vibrant, reverberating life, who have compelled the attention, evoked the sympathy, deserved the repulsion, stimulated the thoughts of readers — over centuries in many cases. Robinson Crusoe discovers the footprint on the sand; Emma is rude to Miss Bates; Catherine Earnshaw says 'I am Heathcliff'; Oliver Twist asks for more; Long John Silver breaks out into 'Fifteen men on the dead man's chest'; Lord Jim repeatedly exclaims 'Nothing can touch me'; Paul Morel feels 'dreary and hopeless' between Miriam and Mrs Morel; and Stephen Daedalus tells his friend Cranly 'I will not serve that in which I no longer believe'.

Novelists continually add to the richness of our human experience; they bring before us new topics, new characters, new attitudes. Mr Milligan in this Introduction to the novel in English rightly includes discussion of novelists who do not come from Britain or America, but are writing in English about their own people – their problems and their pleasures – and adding to our common stock of enjoyment and experience in so doing. Achebe's Okonkwo, Robertson Davies's Monica Gall, Janet Frame's Vera Glace, V. S. Naipaul's Mr Biswas, R. K. Narayan's Krishna the Malgudi schoolteacher, or Patrick White's Mrs Flack join the characters created by earlier novelists. They become inhabitants of our village, the village of the English-speaking, English-reading world. Their creators have often been engaged in discovering the nature of national identities: not only have they brought into the novel a lively, fresh, idiosyncratic use of the English language as it has developed in their countries, but they have interpreted attitudes, moral standards and values, all of which may differ from those of their readers, and consequently they often have a powerful, shaping role in influencing ideas both inside and outside their own countries.

Influential novels undoubtedly have always been; but unless reading them is pleasurable, unless they are, ultimately, enjoyable, their survival value is decidedly dubious. Mr Milligan stresses their emotional effect. No novel, he says, has the right to be dull. And no reader should be passive either! In this book Mr Milligan indicates stimulating ways in which readers can increase the pleasure they experience in reading fiction, by responding to the rewarding challenges each novel presents. To do this is to develop an understanding and an appreciation of different kinds of novels written at different times and in different places. It requires us to read critically, and this both deepens our sensibility and increases our capacity for informed and balanced judgement, for engaging fully those intellectual and emotional responses that contribute our enjoyment.

Stirling, 1982   *A. Norman Jeffares*

Preface

There are few novices in the art of novel-reading; even in an age of television reading begins early, and most interested readers of novels have a wealth of experience to draw on if they decide to take a closer look at how novels are written. This book has been written to encourage students to deepen their experience of reading by paying close attention to the language of the novel. It goes beyond 'practical criticism' by suggesting ways of understanding the structure and design of the novel as a whole. It has been written in the belief that close attention to the text not only increases understanding but enhances the pleasure which readers will find in it.

Reading in depth is a valuable skill, but it may lead to an undesirable narrowing of the range of the reader's interest. The novel in English has been enriched by the contributions of novelists in India, in Africa, in America, in Australasia, in the Caribbean and in India. Students of literature in Britain are often too little aware of these writers, while students elsewhere may sometimes fail to remember the links between novels in English written in their own countries and the historical tradition of which they form a part.

No one book can fulfil all of these objectives, but I am deeply grateful to Professor A. N. Jeffares for encouraging me to write this one, which claims to be no more than an introduction to the novel in English. I wish to thank Miss M. W. Prentice and Miss E. McLellan for their patient and cheerful help in producing the typescript. On this occasion, as on others, my wife's good sense and clear judgment have saved me from some errors: for those that remain the responsibility is mine.

University of Stirling.   *Ian Milligan*

Acknowledgements

The author and publishers wish to thank the following who have kindly given permission for the use of copyright material: The Bodley Head Ltd for an extract from *The Great Gatsby* by F. Scott Fitzgerald in *The Bodley Head Scott Fitzgerald*, and with Random House, Inc., for an extract from *Ulysses* by James Joyce; William Heinemann Ltd for an extract from *Things Fall Apart* by Chinua Achebe; Heinemann Educational Books Ltd and Houghton Mifflin Company for an extract from *The Beautyful Ones Are Not Yet Born* by Ayi Kwei Armah, Copyright © 1968 by Ayi Kwei Armah; David Higham Associates Ltd on behalf of R. K. Narayan for an extract from *The English Teacher*; Laurence Pollinger Ltd on behalf of Graham Greene, and Viking Penguin Inc., for an extract from *The End of the Affair*, Copyright © 1951, 1974 and 1979 by Graham Greene; Samuel Selvon for an extract from *The Lonely Londoners*; The Society of Authors as the Literary Representatives of the Estate of James Joyce and Viking Penguin Inc., for an extract from *Finnigan's Wake*, Copyright 1939 by James Joyce and renewed 1967 by George and Lucia Joyce.

Every effort has been made to trace all the copyright holders but if any have been inadvertently overlooked the publishers will be pleased to make the necessary arrangements at the first opportunity.

1 *First Thoughts on Novel-Reading*

Why Read Novels?

Why read novels? One answer is that the novel is the most popular kind of literature, in several senses of the word 'popular'. It is the kind of literature most generally bought and read; it is easily and cheaply available in paperback. Novelists have traditionally set out to arouse the interest of their readers, and to stimulate them in all sorts of ways. The novel has been popular in not being too formal; its author does not have to comply with a rigid set of literary rules. Consequently, although it does not seem too difficult to decide what would count as a novel, it would be much more difficult to offer a definition that would include every example. Novels seem to resemble one another as the members of a family do; all kinds of overlapping similarities persuade us to group them together, despite the many differences that separate them. Perhaps the novel owes its popularity to its capacity to surprise us, to produce an apparently endless number of examples within the same general type. A further reason for the popularity of the novel may be the widely held belief that it does not generally make very heavy demands upon the reader; perhaps it is tempting to believe, as we survey the stock of some paperback bookshop, that it demands nothing much more than a reasonable knowledge of our own language.

Even if these impressions are broadly true, they do not offer an adequate description of the variety and range of this most malleable form. This popular kind of literature has been addressed to many different kinds of audience, even if we limit our study of its history to the first appearance of *Don Quixote*, by the Spanish writer, Miguel de Cervantes Saavedra (1547–1616) in 1605, or to the publication just over one hundred years later of *Robinson Crusoe*, by the Englishman, Daniel Defoe (1660–1731). 'Popularity', after all, is a vague word. It carries with it a sense of inclusiveness, of something acceptable to the majority. But that too is a relative term. How large a population do we have in mind? Novels borrowed from circulating libraries may have been popular with one group in the eighteenth century, and novels serialised in periodicals or issued (like those of Charles Dickens) in monthly parts may have been popular with another in the nineteenth century, but their readership was small in proportion to the number of people who could not read at all or who did not have the leisure to enjoy reading for its own sake. As we know the reading public today is much smaller than the public which enjoys television programmes or buys 'pop' records. In recent years the publishing industry has tried to reach wider and wider markets, so that novels have been written for very large numbers of people. The potential readership of a novel is no longer thought of in terms of the population of one city or one country. Novels are marketed internationally like soap powder or cornflakes. Perhaps it would be rash to assume that this must inevitably affect the quality of the 'product', but it would be naive to believe that it made no difference to our ideas of what novels might be like. It would surely be honest at least to admit that some people read novels because advertisers have persuaded them to do so.

Attitudes towards novel-reading have varied considerably through history. Some of the pleasures of novel-reading have seemed valuable and praiseworthy; others have seemed more doubtful. It is perhaps not surprising that in earlier centuries it was thought to be at best a waste of time, at worst a wicked self-indulgence. It does, after all, lock the reader away in a purely private world which is a strange joint creation of the reader and the text he holds in his hand; to the unsympathetic observer, it may appear to be a passive activity which has no discernible end-product; it might easily look as if the reader was lost in some kind of dream world, if we did not sometimes see the mechanical to-and-fro sweep of his eyes as he scans the page.

In a famous and often-quoted passage in the fifth chapter of *Northanger Abbey* (1818), Jane Austen (1775–1817) describes how Catherine Morland and Isabella Thorpe made friends while on holiday and began to share one another's interests. 'They called each other by their Christian names, were always arm and arm when they walked . . ., and if a rainy morning deprived them of other enjoyments, they . . . shut themselves up, to read novels together.' Just at this point, afraid that some readers of her novels might secretly think novel-reading a waste of time, Jane Austen stops short to say:

Yes, novels; – for I will not adopt that ungenerous and impolitic custom so common with novel writers, of degrading by their contemptuous censure the very performances, to the number of which they are themselves adding – joining with their greatest enemies in bestowing the harshest epithets on such works, and scarcely ever permitting them to be read by their own heroine, who, if she accidentally take up a novel, is sure to turn over its insipid pages with disgust ... there seems almost a general wish of decrying the capacity and undervaluing the labour of the novelist, and of slighting the performances which have only genius, wit and taste to recommend them ... 'And what are you reading, Miss —?' 'Oh! it is only a novel!' replies the young lady; while she lays down her book with affected indifference, or momentary shame. – 'It is only Cecilia, or Camilla, or Belinda;' or, in short, only some work in which the greatest powers of the mind are displayed, in which the most thorough knowledge of human nature, the happiest delineation of its varieties, the liveliest effusions of wit and humour are conveyed to the world in the best chosen language.[1]

But *Northanger Abbey* is a novel about a girl who finds out that novel-reading can be a very dangerous activity. Not all novels display the greatest powers of the mind; not all novels demand that their readers display them. The novels Catherine Morland has read prompt her to fantasise in such a way that she imagines ordinary people are engaged in sinister and disgraceful activities, and she interprets everyday objects and events in grotesquely improbable ways. For all its wit and irony, *Northanger Abbey* contains a finely serious defence of the novel as well as a penetrating study of the possible effects of bad novels on susceptible readers. A contemporary novelist, Iris Murdoch (1919–   ), has written about the dangerous consequences of unrestricted fantasy. In her opinion, the fantasies we entertain in everyday life, like the vain dreams of the milkmaid who carries a pail of milk on her head and thinks of what it will buy her, divert our attention from the realities of life, just as the milkmaid's dreams blind her to the obstacle that trips her up and spills the milk. Fantasy deforms our view of the world, and novels can sometimes be nothing more than the vehicles of our fantasy. According to Miss Murdoch, novels which are truly worth reading help us to see things as they really are. Such a view discriminates between novels on philosophical grounds. Some novels are more worthwhile reading than others because they are more in touch with reality. In this view there are more or less true ways of seeing the world; the greatest artists are those who have patiently looked at the world around them until they have seen it as it really is; the best novels are closest to the truth. Human beings have an extraordinary capacity for projecting on to the things and people which surround them, their own hopes, and desires and fears. Only exceptional people – such as the artist whose work has endured through centuries – have been able to switch off this destructive psychological machine and look steadily outwards until the outlines of a world they have not created from their own wishes has become clear to them. Not all critics would agree with this view; indeed some would consider these ideas naive or irrelevant. Novels, they would say, do not tell us anything about the world. They can interest us only as examples of design; they are intricate, amusing, unexpected literary objects. The best measure of their value is how far they upset the expectations which we had of them, how far they deviate from the average, how strange, exotic, aberrant and abnormal they are in language and construction.

Of course, the ways in which novels have been written have changed as ideas about how we can know the world have changed. Iris Murdoch believes that the great age of the novel was the nineteenth century, the century of realism, of an age when people believed that the world existed quite independently of anyone's knowledge of it and could be described in ways that corresponded to how it was. But the idea that we can share a common world has given place to the belief that each individual sees things from a completely individual point of view and that our verbal reports about the world do not refer to anything beyond themselves. Truth is no longer something held in common; it is relative to the individual. My world is a closed world, known only to me; and yours to you. In describing these private worlds, the novel has often been extraordinary, shocking, bizarre. A third stage in this progressive breaking up of the world of realism and of everyday common sense might be the growing belief that even the private world had no consistency. In that case the world of the novel might be random, irrational, unintelligible, vague. The reader could only regard it as a possible world, a hypothesis developed from an initial idea; it would be a shape, a structure, an invention; a curiously made object whose strange design gave passing pleasure. To the question, 'Why read a novel?' the novelist might reply, 'To see what I can do with words, to admire my skill in making something appear where before there was nothing.'

The most traditional answer to our question, however – in, for example, the defence Jane Austen makes of the novel – is that novels do offer us insight into how people live and suggestions about how to live well. In the past, novels have combined information with instruction; they have been a traveller's guide to unknown places and unfamiliar people bound up with a moralist's set of hints about how we should behave among them. Traditionally, the novel has been a mixture of action and commentary, just as the fables of Aesop, the ancient Greek writer, or the parables which can be found in the Bible contained a moral, or message, as well as a story. It was assumed that listening to the story would give pleasure and that the message would be remembered with the story. Novelists have not been content to be limited by such simple ideas of their aim. *Pilgrim's Progress*, by John Bunyan (1628–1688), is a fiction with just such a plain and urgent message for the reader, but what qualities does it have that prompt us to think of it as a novel? It is when Bunyan shows us vividly realised people talking together and acting together in circumstances which the writer has rendered in striking detail that he impresses us as having the imagination of a novelist, as well as the convictions of a preacher.

If conventional readers of the novel demand that the interest of the story should outstrip the significance of the message – no novel has the right to be dull – others might say that mere story is not enough. The man who wants to tell his friends a joke soon realises that the story is very little by itself; everything depends on how it is told. More and more readers come to see that the interest they find in reading novels is a much less obvious one than listening to a good story or taking away some useful tip on how to behave. They may have come to realise that novelists sometimes have a strong persuasive intention on their readers and may use all the available resources of language to produce a powerful emotional effect. And we know well enough that feelings may have the force of convictions. We believe things to be the case because we feel that they are so. It may occur to us to wonder how these effects are produced. Since they work below the level of consciousness, it may be useful to be able to spot them because sometimes we may wish to resist them. For others the pleasure may simply lie in seeing how the writer has gone about his work. Just as a sports lover begins to appreciate the art and technique of the volley and the lob, so the student of the novel enjoys watching the strategy and tactics of the novelist.

A reader who starts to be aware of how the story is being told is able to form a view about the design of the book. He may come to see the novel as a kind of loom on which an intricately patterned carpet is being woven. When such a reader opens the book, the machine begins to turn and the carpet, which has all the magical properties of these flying carpets of Arabian fairy-tale, begins to emerge. The carpet is made of words, not of wool, of words specially chosen for their texture and character and colour – specially chosen, that is, for the design that is to appear on it. We do not know, as the carpet emerges, just how the design will be completed, but we can form our own guess as the work goes on. Behind the loom stands the weaver, who is also the designer. Everything we see as the loom works on has been fashioned by him. When the loom stops, when the book is finally closed, we shall have had the special pleasure of seeing what the design of the whole has been. It is just this sense of completeness, of the coherence and harmony of every part that has made the novel worth reading. Sometimes, as in Dickens's final novel, *The Mystery of Edwin Drood* (1871), the novelist has died before his design was complete, leaving a teasing, insoluble puzzle. For, however much we might be able to admire the pattern of the work after it is complete, who but the author could have the power of imagination and of language which would bring the work to a conclusion?

Of course, novels are not carpets, words are not bits of wool. It makes no sense to ask of a carpet, 'Is it true? Does it have anything to say?' but these do not seem to be nonsensical questions to ask of a novel. Yet the analogy is not totally false, provided it is not pressed too far. Looking at a carpet or a picture is not a passive activity; the pattern has to be grasped by an active effort of mind. Understanding the pattern of a novel is no less active a process. The implications of words and the endless variety of their shades of meaning make the material of which the novel is composed seem much more complex than what is available to the designer of the carpet or tapestry. Words have complex histories; they take some impression from all the circumstances in which they have been used. Although their forms may have changed slowly through centuries, their meanings have been subtly and silently adapted to rapid changes in society. (Of course, every student of language knows that a change in the very forms of words can sometimes occur very rapidly too.) Words such as 'honour', 'virtue', 'obedience', 'heroism', 'manliness', or 'gentility' can scarcely be understood without a knowledge of the ways in which men and women of different generations have used them. What is true of words is also true of the kind of sentences in which they have been arranged. Each region, each historical period has its own way of putting things, and each man or woman has used the styles available at that time or place in a distinctively individual way. To read a novel *properly* (and now we are dealing for a moment with the how rather than the why of novel-reading) we have to be prepared to learn its language, whether it be the language of the author's time and place or the language he has made for himself out of what was available to him at the time. An extreme and startling example of this homely truism can be drawn from *Finnegans Wake*, the novel written by James Joyce (1882–1941) in his variety of twentieth-century English. Consider, for example, the following sentences:

> Margaritomancy! Hyacinthinous pervinciveness. Flowers. A cloud. But Bruto and Cassio are ware only of trifid tongues the whispered wilfulness, ('tis demonal!) and shadows shadows multiplicating (il folsoletto nel falsoletto con fazzolotto dal fuzzolezzo), totients quotients, they tackle their quarrel. Sickamoor's so woful sally. Ancient's aerger. And eachway bothwise glory signs.[2]

Some novels, clearly, are not meant to be popular!

Novels, then, are exciting machines (verbal machines) which transport their readers in space and time. They challenge us to meet the unfamiliar. They offer us a share in the pleasure of making because the designs they consist of are not simply there to be seen; they have to be understood, constructed, recreated by the reader out of the materials and according to the patterns which the fabric of their language contains – or conceals. When we become expert readers, we may begin to see some flaws in the workmanship or in the coherence of the design itself. But as beginning students our first task is to become aware of the pattern of meanings which can be discerned in the novel we are studying. It is only with practice and experience that we shall begin to see that the flood of books we call novels have features in common which allow us to group them together. Each novel has its own pattern, but as our experience widens we may begin to identify patterns running through the history of the form as a whole. These patterns cannot be assembled into a grand design, but the forms of fiction, the ways in which stories have been told, have their own history. An understanding of that historical pattern, haphazard and fragmentary as it may be, does give us some insight into the forms of life which literate societies have evolved in history, some awareness of their predominant interests, and of the myths and guiding principles which have sustained them.

What Novels Should We Read?

The simple answer is whatever pleases us, and if this is too simple it contains an essential hint. Understanding and enjoyment surely do go together when the *study* of any art form or leisure pursuit is concerned rather than the mere practice of it. What we are called upon to understand is the nature of the source of our enjoyment. As our understanding increases, so too, we hope, will our enjoyment. A completely unintelligible task freezes enjoyment and extinguishes interest: solving a puzzle can give pleasure in itself, but there is no pleasure in being thoroughly baffled. Reading novels is meant to be fun, although fun can involve, as everyone knows, hard work and difficulty. We must, however, occasionally experience the exhilaration of success if the difficulties we might sometimes encounter are to be overcome with pleasure. Some of the novels you might want to study – or which you may have to study – may be difficult, difficult even to read through. This should not be an insuperable problem if you have been able to find others that offer no problems – novels which you know you really enjoy. Novel-reading, to offer another metaphor, can be a bit like rock-climbing; the literary ascents can range from the easy to the severe. Get plenty of practice on the lower slopes even if you occasionally suspect you are reading rubbish: that dawning suspicion may be the beginning of critical wisdom. Do not omit the detective story, the romance, the work of science fiction, the escapist adventure. Those best fitted to study the novel, we might think, are those who have enjoyed reading novels. Youthful hours with the novels of P. G. Wodehouse (1881–1973) may turn out to have laid down a valuable stock of knowledge about what a literary man can do with language. If you have read what has given you pleasure, you will be able to reflect upon your own experience, to ask what has pleased you and try to discover what its source has been in the novel itself. You will also have a stock of literary experience to which you can begin to assimilate later novels you may be asked to read, some earlier experience with which the new can be compared. Try not to fall into the mistake of keeping the two categories apart, of distinguishing 'the novels you like' from 'the novels you have to read'. If you find yourself in that position, you have failed to assimilate the reading you see as a task, and what is worse, you may be failing to use the insights you have gained from the reading you have liked.

Nothing can take the place of extensive reading. The history of the European and American novel gives us an endless supply of reading material, and the novel in English is now a world-wide phenomenon. In this book, which concentrates on the study of the form, five novels in particular have been chosen to give a sense of the diversity of the novel-family and some sense of its evolution in time. They are *Pride and Prejudice* (1813) by Jane Austen (1775–1817), *Wuthering Heights* (1847) by Emily Brontë (1818–1848), *Great Expectations* (1861) by Charles Dickens (1812–1870), *Tess of the d'Urbervilles* (1891) by Thomas Hardy (1840–1928) and *The Great Gatsby* (1925) by F. Scott Fitzgerald (1896–1940). Each of these novels is well worth studying, and they are often set as texts for study in examinations in schools and colleges. The first four of these writers have written novels which are among the best-known and most-discussed in nineteenth-century English fiction; the fifth is the work of an American writer who displays some of the new developments in novel writing in the twentieth century. Jane Austen is one of the assured classical writers of fiction, each of whose works is distinctive and memorable. Although she wrote only a small number of novels – some half-dozen in all – they were written with a careful craftsmanship which has ensured her a readership in every generation since they were first produced. Her novels are worth reading and re-reading because they are achievements, unsurpassable in their way, which exhibit some of the most fundamental features of the art of the novelist. Emily Brontë, by contrast, published only one novel, *Wuthering Heights*: this is notable for its force and energy, and because of the strange mixture of surface simplicity and underlying complexity with which it is written. It is astonishing that a work of such passionate intensity should have been so carefully planned. *Wuthering Heights* occupies a very different place in the history of the novel from that of the novels of Jane Austen: it opens up completely new territory and deals with material and settings of a strikingly different kind. Charles Dickens shares some qualities with Emily Brontë. Like her, he deals with areas of human experience which were not explored by Jane Austen; he is in touch with the eccentricities of childish imagination, and with the world of dream and fantasy, to which Jane Austen was less sympathetic; he was able to explore a wide range of social experience, and he is aware of the conflicts which arise for the writer when he or she attempts to convey side by side the inner world of imagination and the outer world of 'real life'. Thomas Hardy was as much poet as novelist; in his novels we can see very vividly how the methods of poetic writing may be applied to the writing of novels, and in particular how unnoticed patterns of repeated imagery can help to shape the novel and to control the reader's response to it. In Scott Fitzgerald's *The Great Gatsby* we are presented with more difficult problems of interpretation. The author does not openly guide the reader to the point where it is clear how the action and characters are to be judged. The ending is left open: the reader must decide, judge, evaluate for himself.

The novel as we know it today arrived late in literature, so that many writers of novels have been aware of, and have used, themes and techniques used by earlier writers. Travel writers, biographers, historians, letter-writers and dramatists have all contributed something to the novel. English, French, Russian and American novelists from the eighteenth century to the present have been aware of the common tradition of which they have been a part, despite the divergences between them. They have been aware of the complex interrelationships between their own cultures – between France and England, between America and England, between Russia and France – and so on. Each has drawn from the other; each at one time has achieved a position of cultural leadership which made it temporarily a focus for others.

The Widening Circle

In the contemporary world the tradition has passed beyond Europe. As in the past, the relationship between the elements of the pattern, as we see it now world-wide, is complex and often contradictory. National literatures, claiming the right of fully individual self-expression, struggle to escape from a tradition of which they are an inescapable part. The novel in English, like the English language itself, has taken root world-wide: it flourishes in social conditions markedly different from those where it began. Other cultures and other languages may come to seem more significant than the historical contribution of English literature. But a view of the novel and of the language in which it is written which ignored the influence of history would be a poor one. Throughout the world the rate of cultural change is rapid: to be ignorant of the past is to misinterpret the present. The cultural confusion of the present may be reduced if we are able to see through its diversity the patterns of the recent and more distant past. It may be that there is no such thing as human nature, but to read, say, the epic of Gilgamesh, discovered amid the ruins of Nineveh and written on twelve tablets around four thousand years ago, is to be aware that men and women have written over millennia about the limitations of earthly life and about the fears and longings to which it is subject. Difficult as it may be to explore the multitudinous variety of this vanished expression of what it was like to be alive at that time and in that place, it would surely be folly to pretend that we could ignore these voices from the past or that they had nothing to say to the present.

Practically, of course, we must restrict our view. The diverse, flourishing literary world of today has its roots in the experimental writing of more than sixty years ago. The modern novel since the 1920s has been dominated by American writers. F. Scott Fitzgerald and Ernest Hemingway (1899–1961) wrote of the experience of being American and of growing up in America, in prose which had an accent and character of its own. Many of these American writers found their individual voice in Europe: in their sense of difference amidst foreign surroundings they discovered an identity of their own. The novels of William Faulkner (1897–1962) were complex and daring experiments in the art of narrative which carried forward the work of James Joyce, and yet at the same time made modern techniques more accessible to ordinary readers. *The Sound and the Fury* (1929), *As I Lay Dying* (1930), *Light in August* (1932) and *Absalom, Absalom!* (1936) are rich, complex, sometimes comic novels which employ a remarkable repertoire of linguistic skills to suggest the variety of human speech and character and the complexity of human history, depending as it does on the fragmentary perceptions of a host of conflicting witnesses. Faulkner's techniques of multiple narration and shifting point of view have passed into the common technical equipment used alike by novelists and film-makers. *Why Are We So Blest* (1972) by the Ghanaian writer, Ayi Kwei Armah (1939–   ), is only one example of a novel which makes contemporary use of techniques pioneered by Faulkner and others.

The vitality of the American novel demonstrates the capacity of this form of literature to reflect the consciousness of widely different groups. It has embraced black writers, such as Richard Wright (1908–60) and Ralph Ellison (1914–   ), Jewish writers, such as Saul Bellow

(1915–   ), Bernard Malamud (1914–   ) and Philip Roth (1933–   ), as well as writers, such as John Barth (1930–   ) and Thomas Pynchon (1937–   ), whose novels are learned, difficult, funny and fantastical attempts to explore the ambiguous relationship between writing and reality.

The diversity of the novel can also be seen in the many other writers in English who live and work in Africa, the West Indies, India, Australia and New Zealand. Africa has developed a strong, independent and varied literary tradition. Novels such as *Things Fall Apart* (1958), *Arrow of God* (1964) and *A Man of the People* (1966) by the Nigerian writer, Chinua Achebe (1930–   ) have achieved world-wide recognition for their sensitive sociological insight and their subtlety of form. Cyprian Ekwensi (1921–   ) has written of the garish lives of people in new and developing city environments. Amos Tutuola (1920–   ) has woven Nigerian folk tales into a weird and delightful tapestry of idiosyncratic English prose. The Kenyan writer, Ngugi wa Thiong'o (1938–   ) has written novels about the modern history of his country in a plain style whose simplicity carries great depth of feeling. White South African writers have written powerfully about the beauty and the conflicts of their country. Outstanding among them is Nadine Gordimer (1923–   ), whose progress as a writer shows a striking development from the relatively straightforward sociological interest of *A World of Strangers* (1958) to the complex mythical intensity of *The Conservationist* (1975). The West Indian novel has achieved in the works of Edgar Mittelholzer (1909–65), George Lamming (1927–   ), Wilson Harris (1921–   ), Samuel Selvon (1923–   ) and V. S. Naipaul (1932–   ) a richness and variety equal to the diversity of the complex society about which they have written. In Australia, a long tradition of writing has produced two major novelists, 'Henry Handel Richardson' (Ethel Florence Richardson, 1870–1946) and Patrick White (1912–   ). The Indian novels of R. K. Narayan (1907–   ) have a humanity, humour, style and breadth of sympathy which give them a special place in the affection of their readers.

Here then is a tradition of writing which, starting from a common stem, has taken separate root in strikingly different cultural circumstances throughout the civilised world. The beginnings of its development, however, may be found in works that were written between, say, 1740 and 1840; by 1940, we may say, the developments which we might think of as specially modern, and which still characterise much of contemporary fiction, have all taken place. For students of fiction in

English the work of the two centuries between 1740 and 1940 is of the greatest significance. The novels which have been selected for special comment here offer a thumbnail sketch of the form of fiction and serve as a useful fund of material to illustrate the more general themes which will be pursued in the chapters that follow.

2 Some Elements of Fiction

What is a Novel?

Even when we know perfectly well what a thing is, we may have problems in defining it. Indeed it may well be that definitions are more of a hindrance than a help; they limit unnecessarily what can be accommodated under a handy general label. The aim of this chapter is not to offer a definition of the novel, but to sketch a recognisable portrait of it (if so stable a metaphor is appropriate to such a wayward phenomenon), and to show how it relates to a group of quite separate literary entities, to which, nevertheless, it has some affinity. The novel, we may say, changing the metaphor abruptly, is a carefully constructed magpie's nest into which all sorts of material have been introduced. One way to begin a study of the novel is to look at some of the stuff that the novelist has taken over for his own purposes. Many materials, we are told, go to form a magpie's nest — stout sticks, turf and clay, bits of cloth of various colours, a button, a shining milk-top. But as the magpie uses them, they lose their original function and become part of the fabric of its elaborate nest. Something of the same sort has happened to the literary elements which novelists have taken over to fashion into their novels. Sometimes, like the builders of human dwelling-houses, they have taken their materials from literary structures which have long fallen into decay.

What novels have in common is that they are works of fiction, written in prose and of a fairly considerable length. The English novelist, E. M. Forster (1879–1970), said they should be more than 50,000 words in length, that is not less than the length of the book you are reading now. But length alone is not much help as a defining characteristic; it is only of some value when we want to distinguish between different kinds of fiction, when we find we need terms to distinguish the novel from the short story or from the *novella*, a form which in English is called, awkwardly enough, the long short-story.

The word 'novella' (an Italian word meaning 'new little thing'), from which the English word 'novel' is derived, is associated with one of the founders of the kind of writing which developed into the modern novel. Giovanni Boccaccio (1313–75) was urged unsuccessfully by his father to take up a business career, but he turned instead to the study of literature when he entered the service of the king of Naples. He wrote poems in courtly and classical style, but in middle life he wrote his *Decameron* (1348–53), a collection of one hundred witty and sometimes scandalous tales which are supposed to be told by a group of young people during a period of enforced seclusion at a time of plague. In these stories human beings are represented as a mixture of follies, vices and tender feelings. Boccaccio turned away from mythology and tales of idealised human behaviour. In the *Decameron* life was presented with a sharp immediacy which has not always been accept-able to the taste of later centuries.

In most European languages the term for the novel is 'roman', which derives from the mediaeval *romance*. This was a kind of narrative, written in the native tongue of the romancer, as opposed to the Latin of the classical scholar, which dealt with the chivalric interests of a courtly society; it was concerned usually with the quest of a knight undertaken to gain a lady's favour; it told of tournaments and of the slaying of dragons and monsters; it mixed the human and the miraculous, allowing the human world to be interpenetrated by the worlds of magic, sorcery and fairy land. The tradition of the novel has always represented a reaction against tales of this kind, but perhaps it is more accurate to see in its history a pendulum movement between two extremes represented by the realistic novella of Boccaccio and the romance, which for English readers may best be identified by a reference to those legends of King Arthur, first collected by the fifteenth-century writer, Sir Thomas Malory (?–1471), in his *Morte d'Arthur* (1485).

In fact the question of what is 'real' has been a constant preoccu-pation of the novelist. One of the greatest of them, the Spanish writer Miguel de Cervantes Saavedra (1547–1616), whose *Don Quixote* represents another landmark in the history of the novel, plays constantly with the idea that the 'real' and the 'fictitious' are difficult to disentangle. Don Quixote's mind and character have, of course, been formed by the romances of chivalry which portrayed life as a chronicle of the adventures of high-mettled heroes whose exploits were dedicated to the unattainable princesses who inspired them. But Cervantes' novel is much more than a satire of such an unworldly view of human nature; it is also a meditation on the character of prose fiction. In Cervantes' view written language has the capacity for creating a reality of its own. Since the hero of the novel lives in a world of fantasy which has been created by the tales of adventure to which he has been addicted, the point of Cervantes' novel is to show how inappropriate his behaviour is in the world of everyday life. But Cervantes makes it clear that our idea of what is acceptable is very largely a convention. The line between an account which is 'fictitious' and one which is 'real' may be difficult to draw. The aim of the writer may be to represent reality, but the medium he uses to do this is language, and there is no way in which happenings in the real world can be represented in language without distortion.

From another point of view, fiction has not been easy to distinguish from reality because many pieces of fiction claimed all the appearance and credentials of reality. Novels were disguised as histories or autobiographies; novelists such as Daniel Defoe were at pains to present their fictions as authentic accounts of the real-life adventures of living people. Defoe's novel, *The Fortunes and Misfortunes of the Famous Moll Flanders* (1721), was (we are told on the title-page) 'written from her own memorandums'. Such a tale was not easily distinguished from another book, wrongly supposed to have been written by Defoe, whose title-page reads as follows: 'The life and adventures of Mrs. Christian Davies,/commonly called/Mother Ross;/who, in several campaigns/ under King William/and the/Late Duke of Marlborough,/In the Quality of/A Foot Soldier and Dragoon,/Gave many signal Proofs of an un-parallel'd Courage and personal Bravery/Taken from her own mouth when/A Pensioner of Chelsea Hospital,/And known to be true by Many who were engaged in those great scenes of Action'.

Again, how do we distinguish such a book from that entitled *Travels into Several Remote Nations of the World* by Lemuel Gulliver, first a surgeon and then a captain of several ships? This book was published with an introductory letter from Captain Gulliver to his cousin Sympson who was supposed to be its publisher, and by a note from the publisher to the reader from Richard Sympson himself. Now we are easily able to identify *Gulliver's Travels* (1726) as a fiction written by the English satirical writer, Jonathan Swift (1667–1745), but it came before its original public disguised as an account of Captain Gulliver's travels, as authentic as the later ones of Captain James Cooke. Now we know it is a piece of fiction, but that does not necessarily mean that it is a novel. Not all fictions, even of the required length, are novels.

(a) *The Novel as History*

The first element of the structure of a novel is 'story' or 'narrative', but what notion do we have of 'story'? The simplest idea of it is a connected series of events: A happens, then B, then C. The nearest we can come to this bare recital of events can be found in some of the reports we find in chronicles written by monks at the time of the invasion of the Danish marauders who came to England in the ninth century AD. Here is a brief extract from one of them:

> Now came the Danish army to Reading in Wessex, and about three nights afterwards the two earls rode up. There the noble Aethelwulf met them on English soil and fought against them, and won the victory. About four nights later King Ethered and his brother Alfred led their great army to Reading and fought with the invaders; and there was great slaughter on both sides, and Earl Aethelwulf was killed; and the Danes were the victors.
>
> About four nights later King Ethered and his brother Alfred fought against the whole enemy force at Aeshdown. And the enemy were in two groups; in one group were Backsecg and Halfdene, the heathen kings, and in the other were the earls. Ethered fought against the king's troops, and King Backsecg was killed; his brother Alfred fought against the earls' men, and Sidroc the elder and Sidroc the younger were killed, and Earls Osbearn and Freyn and Harold were killed; and both armies were put to flight and many thousands were killed, and the fighting went on until darkness fell.[1]

In this account we have little more than a recital of facts in chronological order. There is no comment on the facts that are recorded; victories are reported as impartially as defeats. There is a complete absence of 'colour'; there is no detail, no sense of involvement, no description of the personalities or characteristics of the men who are fighting. We certainly do not have any reason to suppose that we are reading the account of someone who knew about the excitement or danger of being a soldier. We may contrast that piece with a much later description of a battle. Here is an account of the battle of Crecy which was fought between the French and the English in 1436. It has been translated from the French of Sir John Froissart, who was a boy of eight when the battle was fought.

When the French king saw the Englishmen, his face changed colour, and he said to his marshals, 'Make the Genoese archers go on ahead, and begin the battle in the name of God and St. Denis'. There were about fifteen thousand Genoese bowmen, but they were so weary of going on foot that day — they had travelled six leagues carrying their crossbows — that they had said to their marshals, 'We are not fit to fight today: we are not in a state to do any great deeds of arms; we are more in need of rest'. When the Duke of Alençon heard of this he said, 'A man should count himself lucky to be in charge of such a pack of rascals, who faint and fail in time of greatest need'. That day there was a heavy fall of rain, and an eclipse of the sun, accompanied with terrible thunder; before the rain, a great number of crows came flying over both armies, terrified by the coming storm. Then the air began to clear and the sun came out — it shone right into the eyes of the French, though the English had it on their backs. When the Genoese were assembled and began to advance, they leaped in the air and shouted, hoping to make the English afraid, but they stood still and did not move at all; then the Genoese gave another leap and a terrifying shout, but the English stood firm; they leapt and shouted a third time and advanced into range; then they released their crossbows. At that moment the English archers took one pace forward and let fly their arrows in such a thick shower that it seemed as if it was snowing. When the Genoese felt the arrows penetrating their heads, arms and breasts, many of them threw down their crossbows, cut the strings of their bows and retreated in disorder. When the French king saw them fleeing, he said, 'Kill these cowards; they will only get in our way now'. Then you should have seen the men-of-arms dash in among them and kill a great many of them. And still the Englishmen shot where they saw the crowds were thickest; their arrows ran into the men-of-arms and their horses; many men and horses among the Genoese fell, and when they were down they could not get up again. Besides, there were so many men jostling there that they knocked one another down. Among the Englishmen there were some scoundrels who went on foot with long knives; they went among the men of arms and murdered many who were lying on the ground — earls, barons, knights and squires. The king of the English was displeased at this, since he had rather they had been taken prisoner.[2]

Here we have a far greater sense of involvement in the events that are being reported. We find here what is missing in the earlier chronicle — those details which give a sense of fullness and authenticity to the story. Accumulation of detail helps to convince us of the truth of what we are being told. There is also a sense of coherence about the account which persuades us of its truth. The Italian crossbowmen were tired, they had the sun in their eyes, their tactics failed to frighten the English — no wonder they began to run away. Other details suggest there was some disharmony between the Genoese bowmen and their French officers. There is just a hint that the weather — and, perhaps, the omens — were against them. But though the English are praised for their steadiness, their behaviour was not praiseworthy in every respect. Here, we may think, is a narrator whose impartiality we can trust. The reported words of the soldiers and of their commanders add weight to our sense that here is a story we can believe. Sir John Froissart, who wrote this account, was only eight when the battle of Crecy took place. No doubt he relied for his story on people who had been there, but what we have been admiring is not his factual accuracy (which we have no means of testing) but his skill as a writer. In Froissart's account, whether it be 'true' or not, there is more than a chronological ordering of events; implicitly, the details given support the explanation for the outcome of the fighting, which lies not far hidden below the surface of the narrative. We are in the hands of someone who appreciates soldierly skills and who can make judgements about human behaviour. Perhaps there is also a feature of the narration which Sir John Froissart was not entirely aware of: it is written very much from the standpoint of an aristocratic observer. The kings, whether French or English, are men of nobler character than the soldiers they command. Implicitly, there is a ranking of the participants from kings and noblemen on horseback to the foot soldiers on whom indeed the outcome of the battle depended, but who were not to be depended on. The account is written from a position of close sympathy with those who occupied the top of this hierarchy of moral worth. Froissart's narrative not only has logical coherence and explanatory power, it has a point of view.

Perhaps we can say that all discourse which claims to tell us what happened has something fictitious about it. Even when it claims to be an account of historical events, there is a process of selection which must depend on the skills of the author. Keenness of vision and retentiveness of memory will not be enough to produce a convincing narrative without an understanding of what is going on and an ability to bring confused and complex events into order. The convincingness of a narrative depends upon its explanatory power, and explanations are theories supported by corroborative detail. In Cervantes' *Don Quixote* one episode tells of the knight's descent into a hole in the ground which he believes to be the cave of the enchanter, Montesinos. After Don Quixote has recounted what he alleged he had seen there, the narrator makes the following comment:

> I cannot persuade myself that all that is written in the previous chapter literally happened to the valorous Don Quixote. The reason is that all the adventures till now have been feasible and probable, but this one of the cave I can find no way of accepting as true, for it exceeds all reasonable bounds. But I cannot possibly suppose that Don Quixote, who was the most truthful gentleman and the noblest knight of his age, could be lying; for even if he were riddled with arrows he would not tell a lie. Besides, if I consider the minute and circumstantial details he entered into, it seems an even greater impossibility that he could have manufactured such a great mass of extravagance in so short a time. So if this adventure seems apocryphal, it is not I that am to blame, for I write it down without affirming its truth or falsehood.[3]

We will pass over for the moment the dimension added here by the presence of a commentator on the story which is being told. The key sentence in the commentary above is the one which reads, 'Besides, if I consider the minute and circumstantial details he entered into, it seems an even greater impossibility that he could have manufactured such a great mass of extravagance in so short a time.' One of the criteria of the novel is its apparent adherence to truth, or at least its probability. It signifies its truthfulness by its wealth of corroborative detail. A fundamental building material out of which novels are made is a narrative that claims to be factual and which contains internal evidence of an appropriate kind to convince readers of its truth. One of the tests of the novel as we know it is probability; another is consistency. Novels, if they are to be effective, must be coherent.

It is not surprising, perhaps, that the rise of the novel coincided with the development in Europe of the scientific attitude. Cervantes' novel,

Don Quixote, which has already been mentioned, was written in two parts, the first published in 1605, the second, a continuation of the first, in 1615. This novel looks backwards to a past where narratives were untrammelled by questions of probability: earlier romances had been enjoyed because they recounted feats which were impossible; incredible adventures, tales of magic, of monsters, giants, necromancers, princesses in distress and selfless knights-errant had been their stock-in-trade. In trying to live his own life in accordance with the principles of chivalry and with the expectations of adventures gained from his reading of earlier romances, Don Quixote puts himself and his squire, Sancho Panza, in ridiculous and humiliating situations. And yet Cervantes and his readers prize the old knight because he represents the power of the imagination to think of the world as other than it is, and to transform human life by conceiving it according to rules which are not the product of circumstances, but which come from the power of the human mind to see the world in new and unexpected ways. A modern philosopher might see these two aspects of *Don Quixote* as, on the one hand, the mental resourcefulness to think of things in a variety of ways – as windmills, or giants; as an advancing army, or a flock of sheep – and the experimental, critical turn of mind which tries to find ways of testing its hypotheses. Novels are not just stories; they must bear some relationship to the concepts of truth or of value which the author espouses.

(b) The Novel and the Fable

In the preceding section we have made a distinction between the novel and the romance, the essence of which is that, as opposed to the romance, the events of the novel should be probable. In this section we distinguish between the novel and the fable. It is necessary to make quite clear what we mean by this term, because 'the romantic' and 'the fabulous' may appear to mean much the same thing. Adventures in the romance tradition were fabulous, unbelievable. Green knights had their heads sliced off, and calmly replaced them; incautious poets were spirited off by the fairy queen. The fable referred to here is of a different kind. Traditionally we owe our knowledge of these fables to the Greek slave Aesop (?–564 BC); originally they were stories about animals, and their intention was to offer advice to people on how to behave. They are of the stuff that the proverbs of ordinary life are made of, and may contain as many contradictions. But humble stories of this kind with their explicit intention of teaching a lesson have contributed something to the building material which has gone into the construction of the novel. One of Aesop's fables reads as follows:

A lion, a donkey and a fox joined in partnership to go out hunting. When they had caught a quantity of game, the lion told the donkey to share it out. The donkey divided it into three equal parts and told the lion to choose one. At this the lion was angry: he fell on the donkey and killed him. Then he asked the fox to make the division. The fox made one heap of all the best bits of meat, leaving a few scraps on the other side: then he invited the lion to choose. 'Who taught you to divide things in this way?' asked the lion. 'I learned from what happened to the donkey', replied the fox. The mistakes of others teach us to be wise.[4]

When the French poet, La Fontaine (1621–95), wrote his own versions of these fables for the young son of Louis XIV in 1668, he chose to re-tell a slightly different version of this fable, in which the lion makes his own division of the spoil into four parts and then tells his three partners that he claims the first share because he is king, the second share because he is the strongest, the third share because he is the most daring, and that if anyone claims the fourth share he will kill him. Unlike Aesop, who expresses the point of the fable in its final sentence, La Fontaine leaves the reader to make an interpretation for himself. But the language he uses implies that the story told of animals can be applied to human behaviour; indeed, in some instances, close parallels are suggested with contemporary institutions. The fables of La Fontaine have a satirical edge; his readers could see allusions, if they wished, to social abuses of their own day. As La Fontaine put it in the letter he wrote to the little prince for whom the fables were intended, 'They look childish but these childish things are merely the vehicle of important truths.' According to La Fontaine, reading Aesop's fables caused the seeds of goodness to start germinating in the human soul; they taught people to know themselves.

La Fontaine was willing to compare his work to that of Euclid in geometry: having arrived at definitions of the point, and the line and the surface of the plane, the geometer was able to measure the heavens; in the same way the moralist used the apparently trifling matters treated of in the fables to form human character and shape the judgement of men in the serious business of life. La Fontaine reminds his readers that Truth, in the person of Jesus of Nazareth in the New Testament, spoke in parables. There is no need to remind readers of the power of parables; they are part of the inherited culture of Europe. But most religious leaders have used this form of expression.

Fable and *parable* may be regarded as a sub-group of the more general category of *allegory*. In an allegory the action and the persons involved in it make good sense on one level, but they signify a second order of events and of ideas. An allegory is a fiction which has been organised to demonstrate the truth of an idea that could be quite precisely formulated in a statement.

One of the greatest allegories in English literature is *The Pilgrim's Progress* (1678, 1684) by John Bunyan. It was written to demonstrate a statement which might run as follows: The only worthwhile object in life is to find the way out of a sinful world which leads to the everlasting life promised by the Christian religion. Christian, the central figure of the first part of the allegory, is represented as fleeing from the city of Destruction in search of salvation from the sin and guilt from which he suffers. The story tells how he found his way to the Celestial City, where he and his companions were met by a company of the heavenly host, and given harps to play and crowns to wear. On his way to the City Christian meets many people who influence him with good or bad advice and example. Those he meets have names such as Hopeful, Faithful, Timorous, Ignorance and Talkative, each of them signifying virtues or defects of character which might help the seeker after personal salvation to reach his end. Here is Christian's encounter with Mistrust and Timorous, as they attempt to climb the Hill Difficulty on their way to the City of Zion, that is, the Celestial City, or Heaven:

Now, when he [Christian] was got up to the top of the hill, there came two men running amain; the name of the one was Timorous and of the other Mistrust: to whom Christian said, Sirs, what's the matter? you run the wrong way. Timorous answered, that they were going to the City of Zion, and had got up that difficult place: but, said he, the further we go, the more danger we meet with; wherefore we turned, and are going back again.

Yes, said Mistrust, for just before us lie a couple of lions in the way, whether sleeping or waking we know not; and we could not think, if we came within reach, but they would presently pull us in pieces.

Then said Christian, You make me afraid; but whither shall I fly to be safe? If I go back to my own country, that is prepared for fire and brimstone, and I shall certainly perish there; if I can get to the Celestial City, I am sure to be in safety there: I must venture. To go back is nothing but death; to go forward is fear of death and life everlasting beyond it: I will yet go forward. So Mistrust and Timorous ran down the hill, and Christian went on his way.[5]

The interest for students of the novel is how skilfully Bunyan has conveyed abstract ideas about the problem of persevering in a religious intention, in simple illustrations drawn from everyday life. Though we are never allowed to forget the secondary meaning of his story, it has the vividness that we expect of the novel. But though it is vivid, it is not free. All of its material must exemplify the beliefs which Bunyan holds and which he wants his readers to share. Bunyan comes closest to being a novelist in his demonstrations of psychological states. Consider this allegorised account of a seventeenth-century 'mugging':

Then said Christian to his fellow, Now I call to remembrance that which was told me of a thing that happened to a good man hereabout. The name of that man was Little-faith; but a good man, and he dwelt in the town of Sincere ... and this Little-faith, going on pilgrimage, as we do now, chanced to sit down [in a lane called Deadman's Lane] and sleep. Now there happened at that time to come down the lane from Broadway-gate three sturdy rogues, and their names were Faint-heart, Mistrust, and Guilt, three brothers; and they espying Little-faith where he was, came galloping up with speed. Now the good man was just awakened from his sleep, and was getting up to go on his journey. So they all came up to him, and with threatening language bid him stand. At this Little-faith looked as white as a sheet, and had neither power to fight nor fly. Then said Faint-heart, Deliver thy purse; but he making no haste to do it (for he was loath to lose his money), Mistrust ran up to him, and thrusting his hand into his pocket, pulled out thence a bag of silver. Then he cried out, 'Thieves, thieves!' With that Guilt, with a great club that was in his hand, struck Little-faith on the head, and with that blow felled him flat to the ground, where he lay bleeding as one that would bleed to death. All this while the thieves stood by. But at last, hearing that some were upon the road, and fearing lest it should be one Great-grace that dwells in the town of Good-confidence, they betook themselves to their heels and left this good man to shift for himself. Now, after a while, Little-faith came to himself, and getting up, made shift to scramble on his way.[6]

What we have here is an allegory of a psychological state. The man who is not confident in his own belief, no matter how sincerely it is held, is easily overcome by the crippling effect of timidity and self-doubt and guilt. Guilt's 'great club' most effectively renders the sense of depression and incapacity that this state of mind can inflict on those who suffer from it.

Pilgrim's Progress cannot be called a novel: Bunyan's intention is too firmly fixed upon his didactic purpose to allow the freedom that seems essential to the novel proper, but fable, parable and allegory have contributed much to the novel. In the eighteenth and nineteenth centuries the names of characters in novels often indicate something of their temperament and role in the novel. In the twentieth century George Orwell (1903–50) in *Animal Farm* expanded the possibilities of the animal fable in a way which demonstrated its capacity for allegorical and satirical treatment. Here then is another of the basic building materials for the novel. Novelists have been aware of the possibility of manipulating their fictions so that they refer to persons, situations and concepts beyond the individual cases with which they deal. Novelists, like story-tellers in all ages and cultures, have used their narratives to instruct and persuade, to form opinion and offer examples of how life might be lived. Part of the primary aim of novelists has been a concern to explore the principles and moral values which guide the lives of their characters.

(c) *The Novel and the Character*

A persistent aim in the history of psychology has been the attempt to describe recurrent patterns of human behaviour, to describe and classify people according to their types. How convenient it would be if we could reduce the variety and diversity of humanity to a basic group of characteristic features which might combine in complex ways to give us the people we see around us in everyday life. One well-known modern psychologist has tried to do this by describing certain characteristic types of bodily structure from which, he believes, patterns of human behaviour can be inferred. The Swiss psychologist, Jung (1875–1961), drew a broad distinction between men and women who were extroverts and those who were introverts; the Austrian, Sigmund Freud (1856–1939), found the basic patterns of behaviour and attitude had their foundation in the early up-bringing of the child and, in particular, in the way his early bodily needs had been satisfied by his mother. Earlier physicians, influential in the Middle Ages, who drew their knowledge from the medical treatises of Greek and Roman writers, believed that the predominant type of mixture of the fluids in one's body — the humours, as they called them — determined one's characteristic outlook on the world.

An interest in character can be seen as early as the ancient Greek writer, Theophrastus, who in 319 BC wrote a little book called *The Characters*. In it he offers little sketches of types he had known. His aim was didactic: Theophrastus wanted to help young men to choose their friends and to distinguish good from evil companions. Here he is on Talkativeness:

> Talkativeness is conversation that is irrelevant, or long and unconsidered; the talkative man is one that will sit down close beside somebody he does not know, and begin to talk with a speech in praise of his own wife; then he will recount a dream he had the night before, and then tell dish by dish what he had for supper. As he warms to his work, he will remark that we are by no means the men we were, that the price of wheat has gone down and that there are a great many strangers in town . . . Next he will suggest that the crops would be all the better for some more rain; he will tell you what he is going to grow on his farm next year, adding that it is hard to make both ends meet. He will tell you that Damippus' torch was the largest set up at the Mysteries (which everyone knows already), and how many pillars there are in the Hall of Music, and 'I vomited yesterday' and 'What day is it today?' . . . And if you let him go on he will never stop.[7]

This is a second-hand impression of the character of the man who talks too much without having anything to say. Only at the end of the sketch do we overhear something of what he had to say. Theophrastus is describing a type: contrast Dickens's presentation of an example of the same kind of character in his novel *Little Dorrit*. Arthur Clennam, the principal male character, meets Flora Finching, someone he had been fond of when they were both younger:

'You mustn't think of going yet', said Flora – Arthur had looked at his hat, being in a ludicrous dismay and not knowing what to do: 'you could never be so unkind as to think of going, Arthur – I mean Mr. Arthur – or I suppose Mr. Clennam would be far more proper – but I am sure I don't know what I am saying – without a word about the dear old days gone forever, when I come to think of it I dare say it would be much better not to speak of them and it's highly probable that you have some more agreeable engagement and pray let Me be the last person in the world to interfere with it though there *was* a time, but I am running into nonsense again.'

Was it possible that Flora could have been such a chatterer in the days she referred to? Could there have been anything like her present disjointed volubility in the fascinations that had captivated him?

'Indeed I have little doubt', said Flora, running on with astonishing speed, and pointing her conversations with nothing but commas, and very few of them, 'that you are married to some Chinese lady, being in China so long and being in business and naturally desirous to settle and extend your connection nothing was more likely than that you should propose to a Chinese lady and nothing was more natural I am sure than that the Chinese lady should accept you and think herself very well off too, I only hope she's not a Pagodian dissenter.'

'I am not', returned Arthur, smiling in spite of himself, 'married to any lady, Flora.'

'Oh good gracious me I hope you never kept yourself a bachelor so long on my account!' tittered Flora; 'but of course you never did why should you, pray don't answer, I don't know where I'm running to, oh do tell me something about the Chinese ladies whether their eyes are really so long and narrow always putting me in mind of mother of pearl fish at cards and do they really wear tails down their back and plaited too or is it only the men, and when they pull their hair so very tight off their foreheads don't they hurt themselves, and why do they stick little bells all over their bridges and temples and hats and things or don't they really do it?' Flora gave him another of her old glances. Instantly she went on again, as if he had spoken in reply for some time.[8]

Readers who wish to find how the conversation developed will have to look it up in Chapter 13 of *Little Dorrit*. Theophrastus presents us with a description of a type which we can still recognise, despite the local references to fourth-century Athens; but whereas Theophrastus describes, Dickens shows us character in action. Flora Finching is not exactly a type. She is the garrulous woman with features of her own which are wholly individual. What is remarkable about her is her unpredictability. Her talkativeness has no rational or even grammatical controls. Her talk allows us an insight into her view of the world which is irrational, exotic, unpredictable, and overgrown — like some domestic vegetable run to seed and producing extravagant forms, unrelated to the normal plant. Dickens focuses in particular on the syntax of Flora's sentences; indeed he draws attention to it himself — she points 'her conversations with nothing but commas, and very few of them' — the only punctuation is when she draws breath. There is no logical sequence to it whatever. There is, of course, a strong emotional under-current which shapes Flora's outpourings. The words she utters are like the leaves and twigs forced along by a powerful wave of water; the under-current in Flora's case is her coy, partly revealed hope that Arthur Clennam is still interested in marrying her.

Character and the language appropriate to it have been a central interest of the literary creator in prose or verse since the earliest period of English literature. In his *Canterbury Tales* (1387–92) Chaucer (*c*. 1340–1400) prefaced his work with a Prologue which offers character-sketches of the people who are to tell stories on the way to Canterbury. In the Prologue he excuses himself for the kind of language he might use by saying that one of the first duties of an author is to be true to the kind of character he is exhibiting and in particular to that character's language. 'Whoever tells a tale as someone else has told it must keep as close to the original language as possible, no matter how grossly or broadly it has been told. If he fails to do this, he will be distorting what he has heard, or making things up, or finding different words.' Clearly Chaucer believed in authenticity, in keeping as close to the original as possible, no matter how embarrassing or unsuitable he might appear to be to polite society. A later critic, John Dryden (1631–1700), asked why it was necessary to introduce such people in the first place. There is clearly an area for debate about the limits of an author's freedom to write whatever he chooses on the grounds of authenticity. But perhaps we might think it a considerable virtue that at this early stage in its history English literature had such a model, or pattern, of breadth and comprehensiveness.

In this section we have considered the relationship and the differences between the kind of character-sketches offered by an essayist and the characters in action presented by novelists. A final example comes from the work of the seventeenth-century writer, John Earle (1600–65), whose book of character summaries was subtitled 'A piece of the world discovered in essays and characters'. Here he is on 'A child':

> He is nature's fresh picture newly drawn in oil, which time, and much handling, dims and defaces. His soul is yet a white paper unscribbled with observations of the world, wherewith, at length, it becomes a blurred note-book. He is purely happy, because he knows no evil, nor hath means by sin to be acquainted with misery. He arrives not at the mischief of being wise, nor endures evils to come, by foreseeing them. He kisses and loves all, and, when the smart of the rod is past, smiles on his beater. . . . He plays yet, like a young 'prentice the first day, and is not come to his task of melancholy. All the language he yet speaks is tears, and they serve him well enough to express his necessity. His hardest labour is his tongue, as if he were loth to use so deceitful an organ; and he is best company with it when he can but prattle. We laugh at his foolish sports, but his game is our earnest; and his drums, rattles and hobby-horses but the emblems and mocking of man's business. His father has writ him as his own little story, wherein he reads those days of his life that he cannot remember, and sighs to see what innocence he has outlived.[9]

Some readers may think this is altogether too pessimistic a view of the likely general development of human lives; others will warm to its depth of experience and keen sensitivity to the inherent limitations of human development, of which small children give no hint and of which they have no intimation. It includes in its sketch of childhood the dimension of time and a consciousness of an historical perspective, which young children do not themselves have. It is this understanding (that development implies complexity, and that complexity is often muddled and incoherent) which justifies Bishop Earle's melancholy view of human nature. His character-sketch is a story in embryo; it is the diagram, where the novel is the picture – a moving picture at that; a fully developed action organised, as one writer has put it, 'so that it introduces characters about whose fate we are made to care, in unstable relationships which are then further complicated until the complication is finally resolved by the removal of the represented instability'.[10] John Earle's character resembles one of those paper Japanese flowers which opens out fully only when dipped in water. His is a general statement of a theme, the kernel of an idea. He is far more concerned with the general features of childhood than with any individualising traits. Indeed, to introduce individual features into his diagram of the sad limitations of human life, which are most poignantly discovered when we consider the life of a child, might weaken the force of his general-isation. The novel, we might think, tests these general statements about human life by carefully analysing individual segments of it, by contrasting general truths and specific examples of human behaviour. What the novelist must ask of John Earle's essay is — how could it be individualised, expanded, developed until we have a distinctly delineated record of an action, which may leave us with a sense of the limitations of human life such as we find in *Great Expectations* (1861), or in George Eliot's *The Mill on the Floss* (1860), or in J. D. Salinger's *The Catcher in the Rye* (1951), in Chinua Achebe's *Things Fall Apart* (1958), or in Ngugi wa Thiong'o's *Weep Not, Child* (1964). What is needed is the conversion of statement into action, of the general into the particular; we require some way of finding that these general conclusions are supported by observation and imagined experience which will ring true when tested against the private experience of those who read it.

3 *The Language of the Novel*

Beginnings

Here is a passage from a novel written by Richard Graves (1715–1804) in 1772. The novel is called *The Spiritual Quixote* and it concerns two characters in particular, Mr Geoffrey Wildgoose and his manservant, Jerry Tugwell, who set off through England to preach Methodism in much the same way as Don Quixote and Sancho Panza had set out to present an example to the world of the virtues of chivalry in Cervantes' novel, published in 1605.

The moon shining very bright, and there being but little night at that time of the year, the two pilgrims pursued their journey, taking the first road they could find which pointed towards Gloucester. They had travelled near a mile, and were now got into a very dark lane, by the side of a wood, and the stillness of the night, in a strange place, raised in Tugwell some ideas of terror, which (notwithstanding his personal valour in rencounters and at fisticuffs) he had in his youth been greatly subject to; and though he pretended now to be above these childish fears, yet he stuck very close to his master, and, with an affected bravery, began to fish out Wildgoose's opinion about ghosts and apparitions.

'Some folks now,' quoth Jerry, 'would be almost afraid to walk by themselves in such a dark lane, at this time of night; but I don't suppose there is any sich thing as spirits now-a-days – do you think there are, Master Wildgoose?' – 'Any such thing as spirits, Jerry? Why, I believe there are no more walk by night than there are by day; and I am partly of the same opinion with a great man, who says, "That goblins and spirits have really no more to do with darkness than with light", and accounts for our terror on these occasions from what he calls "the association of ideas." ' – 'Yes, yes,' says

Tugwell, 'I remember the sociation in the time of the rebellion: our 'squire would not sociate.' – 'No, no, Jerry, what I mean, is the joining things together in our fancy; so that when a child is told by his nurse, of ghosts appearing by night, he shall never be able to separate the notion of spirits from that of darkness, as long as he lives. But though this may account for that particular kind of terror, yet certainly the sense of our being off our guard, when alone in the dark, and ignorant what enemies we may be exposed to, must necessarily make us apprehensive of danger upon those occasions. So that, let a man have never so clear a head to separate ideas, yet I think it almost impossible to be equally calm and easy in darkness and solitude, as we are in the open day-light.'

Tugwell was still as a mouse during this discourse of Wildgoose, though he did not understand a word that was said.[1]

The language of this passage is extraordinarily simple and clear, although it is obvious that it is not written in the English of the twentieth century. The use of present participial phrases ('the moon shining very bright ... there being but little night') at the beginning of the first sentence marks the English as unusual by present-day standards; so do the phrases 'near a mile' and 'they ... were got into'. The first feature of the English seems more formal than would be usual today, the second less so. We would not expect to find the word 'rencounter' in current English. But the reader is easily able to identify what we have here as an extract from a novel. We are being told of an episode which has taken place. It is written in the past tense by an author who is in possession of all the facts about what was supposed to happen. (The reader, of course, knows that the author has created the 'facts': his special skill lies in persuading the reader to forget this.) He does not relate every fact that he may have known (or imagined) about the scene. What matters is that the brightness of the moonlight gives place to the darkness of a lane situated close to a wood (where perhaps unexpected or alarming presences may be lurking). What matters for author and reader is the sequence of words which carries a message of fear: 'gloominess ... stillness ... strange ... terror' followed by the equally evocative 'ghosts ... apparitions ... spirits'. The passage is organised in such a way that we can detect an interplay between its parts so that the final sentence ('Tugwell was still as a mouse ...') seems a fitting climax to this section of the novel as a whole. The various elements of the passage – the novelist's narration, the speech of Tugwell and the speech of his master – are governed by a constant, directed and unified intention of the writer. In this little section of the novel his aim apparently is to raise a laugh at the expense of Jerry Tugwell.

Why, we might ask, does that final line seem amusing? The answer is that it describes Jerry's appearance; the description allows us to deduce that Jerry is frightened. We laugh because his behaviour is such an inappropriate response to what his master has been saying, which, the author tells us, he has not understood. Our laughter is not completely unkind – though over-sensitive readers may feel uneasy at Graves's depiction of Jerry. We are not laughing at his ignorance; we are laughing at the fact that two men in the same situation can be so utterly far apart in feeling as Tugwell and Wildgoose are. It is as incongruous as two singers would be who were singing a duet in different keys.

The author is not simply telling us what happened: he has organised his material so that it reaches a climax in a joke, a pause for laughter, which he has arranged and which we can first share, then analyse and appreciate. The sequence of events – in this case the conversation of the two men and the narrative and commentary of the author – has a pattern, a rhythm, which is appropriately brought to an end (just as a rally in tennis is appropriately brought to an end by a winning or a losing shot). We might even call our little sequence 'dramatic' because the reader has to grasp, without being told explicitly, just what the point of the organised sequence of events is.

But while in some ways the author expects the reader to react appropriately without being told, in other ways he makes his own attitudes to the characters and situation very clear. He makes sly jokes about Jerry (how convincing is his reference to Jerry's bravery, for example); what view will the reader have of a man whose bravery is 'affected'? What do you think of the first sentence he speaks, in the light of what we have been told about the revival of his childish fears, as he walks down this dark lane?

Obviously, the author wants us to be aware of the differences between Jerry and his master: there are differences of understanding – Jerry does not understand the phrase 'association of ideas' – and there are social differences in the kind of speech they use. (You might think that the differences in understanding are very largely social, too.) The author's use of the word 'quoth' to introduce Jerry's first speech may be thought patronising: it is an old-fashioned word which carries a hint of warning that we are about to hear the ill-considered remarks of a rustic. The speech itself has traces of the dialect of a countryman, which traditionally carries comic overtones, but perhaps more important than that is the childish doubt and confusion which Jerry Tugwell shows. Is he not – for a big chap used to fist fights – just a little too reliant on his master's opinions? Does not his use of that word 'Master' suggest a deference which is based on a dim awareness of his own sad state of ignorance? (After all, his very name suggests a deferential tugging at cap or forelock.)

When Wildgoose replies, the author uses the perfectly neutral word 'says', and the reader is treated to a small lecture on how people's minds work. Richard Graves, the author of the novel, tells us in a foot-note that the 'great man' Wildgoose refers to is John Locke (1632–1704), the English philosopher, who introduced the concept of 'the association of ideas' to explain some aspects of the activity of thinking. Wildgoose holds the opinion that a fear of the dark is brought about by 'the association of ideas': children who are told frightening stories of ghosts by their nurse at bed-time will think of ghosts whenever it gets dark. But just as Wildgoose's remarks on this subject become too abstract to follow, the reader is brought back by language full of expressive feeling to Jerry Tugwell who is 'still as a mouse' while his master is talking, and who is clearly far more aware of his own terror than of the meaning of what Wildgoose is saying to him. John Locke and 'the association of ideas' are not brought into the conversation because Graves wants to provide us with information on these matters; they are brought in because Graves uses them as elements in this little drama of incomprehension which he wants to create between Tugwell and Wildgoose.

This little episode in *The Spiritual Quixote* is followed by two ghost-stories – one of them told by Wildgoose, the other by Jerry Tugwell. Notice the differences between them. Here is Wildgoose re-counting something that happened to him at college:

> 'I myself remember, when I first went to the University, I lived in a large chamber, hung with green baize; the bed was placed in a sort of recess, separated from the dining-room by two large folding doors, which were thrown open when I went to bed, to make it more airy. I happened once to wake about midnight, and it being star-light, saw, on the farther side of the room, a tall figure in white, near six feet high. It seemed to have a square cap on its shoulders, but was without a head!' – 'Lord have mercy upon us!' says

Tugwell, laying hold of Wildgoose's skirt; 'yes, without a head! So my grandmother used to say, that ghosts commonly do appear without a head.' 'Well,' continues Wildgoose, 'though I used to laugh at things of this kind, I could not account for this dreadful phenomenon. The more I stared at it, the more I was convinced it was something real. After lying some time, and mustering up my courage, I leaped out of bed, determined to unravel the mystery – when lo! I embraced in my arms a white surplice, which a scholar of the house . . . had hung upon a brass peg, over which I had suspended my square cap, such as they wear in the University!'[2]

Now compare Jerry's story:

'I remember when I was a boy, father had been to fetch the midwife upon your grandfather's mare, old Whitefoot. She was as good a servant as ever went upon four legs. Your grandfather bought her of Old Simon Perkins.' 'Well,' says Wildgoose, 'proceed with your tale!' – 'It was a very dark night,' continues Jerry, 'and father was riding by a lone uninhabited house, at the end of a close lane, as this may be, when he saw strange lights in every window; and when he came into the middle of the lane, vast balls of fire rolled along under his horse's feet: and then the squire's lady, who died in child-bed, drove along in her coach and six, with her child in her arms; and – and – the coachman (it is sartain true) the coachman was without a head – and – '[3]

There are some differences between what is told in each of these stories, and how it is told. Think about some of them for yourself. Some of the differences seem to be connected with what has been said earlier about the use of language as a means of controlling feeling and understanding. Everything Wildgoose says suggests that he is attempting to understand the situation in which he found himself; he felt some fear, but he did not allow this feeling to overwhelm him. What appeared to confront him was mysterious, but it was a mystery that could be unravelled. Wildgoose's world was rational. As he says at the end of his ghost-story, 'Thus, I am convinced, would every story of apparitions have ended . . . if the scared spectator had resolution enough to examine it to the bottom'.

Jerry Tugwell on the other hand imagines himself in his father's position as he tells his story. He feels the fear his father felt. He offers no rational explanation for his father's experience and does not suggest there could be one. But does not the author of this novel suggest a possible explanation for Mr Tugwell senior's experience? Jerry Tugwell's story is not meant to suggest that there are some experiences which cannot be understood rationally; it is rather meant to imply that there will always be some people who are incapable of a rational understanding of things.

In each of these ghost-stories the character who is not telling the story interrupts to make a comment. In each case the comment tells us something about the relationship between the two. Can you see what this relationship is? Does it reinforce what was said earlier about the way the author has presented his two characters? Does it now appear that there are regular differences in the way the author treats Wildgoose and Jerry? Wildgoose's very name suggests that he is a quixotic person – a man who is likely to pursue extravagant ideals – yet on the evidence we have here, the author has endowed him with a strong fund of rational good sense. There is an apparent conflict or contradiction here which perhaps the author aims to resolve during the course of the novel: sensible men do not go on a wild-goose-chase.

Contrast these ghost stories with the following famous scene from *Wuthering Heights*. The narrator has been dreaming and has just woken up to find that the cause of his bad dream was 'merely the branch of a fir-tree that touched my lattice, as the blast wailed by, and rattled its dry cones against the panes.' Here is how the narration resumes:

> I listened doubtingly an instant; detected the disturber, then turned and dozed, and dreamt again; if possible, still more disagreeably than before.
>
> This time, I remembered I was lying in the oak closet, and I heard distinctly the gusty wind, and the driving of the snow; I heard, also, the fir-bough repeat its teasing sound, and ascribed it to the right cause; but it annoyed me so much, that I resolved to silence it, if possible; and, I thought, I rose and endeavoured to unhasp the casement. The hook was soldered into the staple, a circumstance observed by me when awake, but forgotten.
>
> 'I must stop it, nevertheless!' I muttered, knocking my knuckles through the glass, and stretching an arm out to seize the importunate branch: instead of which, my fingers closed on the fingers of a little, ice-cold hand!
>
> The intense horror of nightmare came over me; I tried to draw

back my arm, but the hand clung to it, and a most melancholy voice
sobbed,

'Let me in – let me in!'

'Who are you?' I asked, struggling, meanwhile, to disengage
myself.

'Catherine Linton,' it replied shiveringly . . . 'I'm come home,
I'd lost my way on the moor!'

As it spoke, I discerned, obscurely, a child's face looking through
the window – terror made me cruel; and, finding it useless to
attempt shaking the creature off, I pulled its wrist on to the broken
pane, and rubbed it to and fro till the blood ran down and soaked
the bed clothes: still it wailed, 'Let me in!' and maintained its
tenacious gripe, almost maddening me with fear.[4]

Surely every reader will share the narrator's feeling of horror here:
certainly, we are invited to do so. Nothing protects the reader from
direct contact with the eerie experience. Although we have been told
that it is only a dream, we know how horrifying some dreams can be;
we seem to experience this one directly. Of course, here the story is
told directly by the narrator. The experience begins with reality – the
branch of the fir tree – and turns into terror – the icy hand of the
child. But there is more to the effect of the episode than sheer
experience: notice how the author prepares us for the strange transformation of branch to arm by referring to how the fir-tree 'touched'
the window-pane, how its sound was 'teasing'. The narrator resolves
to 'silence' it, as if it were already alive. The branch is 'importunate',
as if it were already a hand stretched out for help. And as the narrator
touches the branch, it is changed to the fingers of 'a little, ice-cold
hand'. The author's use of language prepares the reader for the change
from inanimate to animate; we experience in language the same
uncanny transformation that the narrator experiences in life. (But of
course only the language exists as the expression of the author's
imaginative intention.) Notice how the author maintains our
uncertainty about the living and the non-living, when the voice is
referred to as 'it', and as 'the creature'. A further horror is that what
seems to be human fails to behave in a human way: despite its loss of
blood, it maintains a tenacious hold on the narrator's arm.

In this passage we are not aware of any authorial voice which
comments on the narrator's story. The tone of the writing directs our
attention to the honesty of the narration, to its careful attempt at

accuracy. The narrator's capacity for doubt, for critical awareness, is established before the beginning of the extraordinary experience which we are told about. Many phrases point to the fact that he is fully in possession of his senses and critical powers – 'I remembered', 'I heard distinctly'. Three levels of time are mentioned in the narration. In the present time he is telling us the story of a past event – the dream – and he also refers to the time before he had gone to sleep. 'I rose and endeavoured to unhasp the casement', we are told, 'The hook was soldered into the staple, a circumstance observed by me when awake, but forgotten.' It is one of those moments in dream when waking life seems on the point of breaking in; even in sleep the dreamer's critical ability has not deserted him and the memory of what he had observed when awake comes to him in the middle of his dream. The narrator's present memory is of a man who, while dreaming, appeared to be fully alert and awake: just as it is difficult to say when the branch becomes a human hand, so it is difficult to tell when dream ends and reality begins. This story, as compared with Wildgoose's story, or Jerry Tugwell's, is much more disturbing. There are no authorial directions to help us to disbelieve it. It is not consciously 'exploded' by the narrator, as Jerry Tugwell's is. Tugwell's incoherence, and his willingness to believe anything, prompt us to disbelieve him; in the dream from *Wuthering Heights* the doubt, the scepticism, the disbelief are all supplied by the narrator, but they do not succeed in challenging the vivid reality of his incredible experience.

By looking carefully at these examples, we can begin to see some of the power of the language of the novelists. Some of the problems of the novelist which our examples have begun to display are not wholly linguistic. Stories can be told, as we know, in film as well as in other language-based media such as radio or on stage. Each has its own techniques of organisation: each has to find means of representing human action, human conversation, human character. Each must find ways of presenting our experience of space and time, our sense of the continuity and discontinuity of human experience, our strange consciousness of being in the world of things, institutions and people which variously resist and yield to our wishes. The medium of the novel is entirely linguistic: if the novelist has plans, strategies, techniques, or intentions which are not explicitly formulated in words, they must be discernible through the language he has chosen for their expression. But to look at the language of small patches of the novel may not be enough. We must look at the way in which the novelist has organised his narrative into chapters and paragraphs; we must be aware of the methods he has used to order his materials and of the patterns into which he has arranged them to draw our attention to the links between them. These topics, however, can be reserved for later chapters. Let us look again in detail at two further passages from well-known novels. The first is a scaring experience which happens to the hero of *Great Expectations* when he is a young boy. The story of *Great Expectations* is told by a single narrator, who tells us his own story in the first person, sharing with us memories of his life from 'disadvantaged' boyhood to 'fortunate' middle-age. The young boy, Pip, has met an escaped convict in the marshes near his home. He insists that the boy brings him a file from his brother-in-law's blacksmith's shop so that he can get rid of the iron chains round his wrists and ankles, and that he should bring him some food ('wittles'). Here is how the convict threatens him:

'You bring me, tomorrow morning early, that file and them wittles. . . . You do it, and you never dare to say a word or dare to make a sign concerning your having seen such a person as me, or any person sumever, and you shall be let to live. You fail, or you go from my words in any partickler, no matter how small it is, and your heart and your liver shall be tore out, roasted and ate. Now, I ain't alone, as you may think I am. There's a young man hid with me, in comparison with which young man I am an Angel. That young man hears the words I speak. That young man has a secret way pecooliar to himself, of getting at a boy, and at his heart, and at his liver. It is in wain for a boy to attempt to hide himself from that young man. A boy may lock his door, may tuck himself up, may draw the clothes over his head, may think himself comfortable and safe, but that young man will softly creep and creep his way to him and tear him open. I am keeping that young man from harming of you at the present moment, with great difficulty. I find it very hard to hold that young man off of your inside. Now, what do you say?'

I said that I would get him the file, and I would get him what broken bits of food I could, and I would come to him at the Battery, early in the morning.

'Say Lord strike you dead if you don't!' said the man.

I said so . . .[5]

'Now,' he pursued, 'you remember what you've undertook, and you remember that young man, and you get home!'

'Goo – Good night, sir,' I faltered.

'Much of that!' said he, glancing about him over the cold wet flat. 'I wish I was a frog. Or a eel!'

At the same time, he hugged his shuddering body in both his arms – clasping himself, as if to hold himself together – and limped towards the low church wall. As I saw him go, picking his way among the nettles, and among the brambles that bound the green mounds, he looked in my young eyes as if he were eluding the hands of the dead people, stretching up cautiously out of their graves, to get a twist upon his ankle and pull him in.

When he came to the low church wall, he got over it, like a man whose legs were numbed and stiff, and then turned round to look for me. When I saw him turning, I set my face towards home, and made the best use of my legs. But presently I looked over my shoulder, and saw him going on again towards the river, still hugging himself in both arms, and picking his way with his sore feet among the great stones dropped into the marshes here and there, for stepping-places when the rains were heavy, or the tide was in.

The marshes were just a long black horizontal line then, as I stopped to look after him; and the river was just another horizontal line, not nearly so broad nor yet so black; and the sky was just a row of long angry red lines and dense black lines intermixed. On the edge of the river I could faintly make out the only two black things in all the prospect that seemed to be standing upright; one of these was the beacon by which the sailors steered – like an unhooped cask upon a pole – an ugly thing when you were near it; the other a gibbet with some chains hanging to it which had once held a pirate. The man was limping on towards this latter, as if he were the pirate come to life, and come down, and going back to hook himself up again. It gave me a terrible turn when I thought so; and as I saw the cattle lifting their heads to gaze after him, I wondered whether they thought so too. I looked all round for the horrible young man, and could see no signs of him. But, now I was frightened again, and ran home without stopping.[6]

Consider for a moment some of the complexities in this piece of writing. Like the episode from *Wuthering Heights* it is written in the first person. The central character of the novel is remembering an event in his childhood. The reader is presented with sentences which suggest that the adult narrator is telling us what happened to him as a boy, but he recalls (or appears to recall) the words which were actually spoken by the people who were taking part in this past event — by himself as a boy, that is, and by the convict speaking, as he did, in terms appropriate to the boy's understanding. We are shown things from the child's point of view. The convict's story of the terrifying young man is designed to frighten the child. We are specifically told that it is in the 'young eyes' of Pip that the convict appears to be 'eluding the hands of the dead people, stretching up cautiously out of their graves, to get a twist upon his ankle and pull him in'. Is there not something both macabre and innocent in this vision, which makes it seem appropriate to childhood? It is both lurid and unlikely, like the stories in horror comics that boys like to read. At the same time, however, there is a shared unspoken joke going on between writer and reader. Pip might believe in the convict's story about the vengeful young man, who is said to be hidden with him, but the reader does not believe in him, surely. Why is this? There is some quality in the writing, some aspect of the convict's warning to Pip which does not ring true to the reader. In the first place it is unlikely that such a young man exists; he sounds like the bogy adults have traditionally talked of when they wanted to frighten children. There is something contrived about the sentences the convict uses to describe him. The repetition of the words 'that young man' decreases, rather than increases, our belief in his existence. The convict's warning to Pip has a formal, almost ritualistic, rhythm. Look at the resemblances between the form of the sentences — 'You do it, and . . . ', 'You fail, and . . . '; look at the elaborate repetitions within the sentences, and the numerous qualifying phrases ('or any person sumever', 'no matter how small it is'). It may remind the reader of the formal patterns and careful qualifications of legal language. The convict's words to Pip hover between the kind of solemn commandment issued by a clergyman and a legal contract. But there is a lack of fit between this formal style and the use of colloquial (and rather uneducated) forms of words such as 'pecooliar' and 'in wain', which tends to undermine the reader's respect for the speaker. But there seems no doubt that the boy believes the story. Here, then, is something the reader is aware of which the character is not. We could say that the adult narrator is aware of this discrepancy, but no special mention is made of that. Perhaps we are aware of three levels on which the story is being told: there is the adult narrator who sometimes shows us how the boy he was reacted to the events he was involved in, but there is a third narrator whom we cannot quite avoid noticing, someone who provides material which is independent of the narrator's boyhood memory and is also independent of the adult narrator's story. There are times, in other words, when Charles Dickens, the author, seems to take over the writing of the story.

The description of how the convict limped away from the boy offers another example of how language can imply suggestions that are not explicitly stated. What feelings do you think the boy has towards the convict as he watches him go? The phrases 'hugged his shuddering body', 'picking his way among the nettles' – notice how these phrases are repeated in the next paragraph, where the convict's 'sore feet' are mentioned – suggest that mixed with the child's fear of the man there was a good deal of pity. When the convict wishes he were 'a frog. Or a eel', there is a suggestion of the inhuman situation in which he has been placed, which is reinforced first by the image of the dead reaching up to catch his ankle, and second by the later image of his going to replace the dead pirate on the empty gibbet – he is in the boy's eyes the dead pirate, come to life for a moment, only to resume his position among the dead. The convict after all is caught here between prison and the likelihood of recapture: he has escaped from a living death and is likely to return to it. As it is, his state is such that even the cattle turn their heads to pity him. Perhaps this suggestion that pity is the natural response to the man's predicament throws light on the identity of the 'young man' the convict has spoken of. If the boy refused to pity such a creature, he might run the risk of being pursued by remorse, a feeling of guilt which might well tear at the insides of those who experienced it.

The most striking use of language in this passage is contained in the final paragraph: the writer makes us vividly aware of the horizontals of marsh, river and sky, harshly coloured in red and black, colours which imply death and misfortune. Against these he has placed two striking verticals – the beacon by which sailors steered, which might appear to suggest light, hope and a mark to aim at (but which, we are told, was 'an ugly thing when you were near it') and the gibbet, which appears to be the destination of the escaped convict. That the convict might be hanged gives Pip 'a terrible turn'. He associates himself with the gaze of the cattle, mild and merciful, it might be thought, in comparison with the attitudes of men to one another and in particular to one thought worthy of punishment.

All of these complex suggestions are implied by the language of this passage. It would be quite inappropriate for the author to make them explicit: the young boy is vaguely aware of some feelings for the convict, but they are subordinate to his immediate feelings of fear: they operate at an unconscious level and are much less fully understood. Dickens has written the passage so that the reader will be aware of much that the central figure, Pip, fails to realise. It is clear that the child is unaware of his feelings; what is not quite clear is how far the adult Pip is aware of them. But since the novel is concerned with the gradual growth of the self-awareness of the main character, and his slow sifting of worthwhile values from false ones, it is appropriate that the narrator should not display too early the maturity which he painfully earns during the course of the novel.

One final small point can be made. The strangely mixed presentation of the convict, part solemn, part ludicrous, may be a deliberately misleading tactic on Dickens's part. This episode is of profound consequence for the rest of the novel. The convict promises that, if Pip brings him the file, he 'shall be let to live'. It is a promise that is handsomely fulfilled since the convict is the source of Pip's later fortune (though Pip does not know it). It is necessary for the development of the novel that this compact between the convict and the boy should be solemnly made. But it is equally crucial for the author that the close relationship between them should be concealed. Perhaps those features of the presentation of the convict which make him seem grotesque, and (at least in part) a figure of fun ('I wish I was a frog. Or a eel') are just enough to prevent us taking him too seriously.

One final passage – from Thomas Hardy's *Tess of the d'Urbervilles* – will show that the language of fiction is able to create meanings that go far beyond the simple depiction of a sequence of events. Tess is a young farm girl whose parents want her to marry a rich man. She and her young brother Abraham have set off at night to deliver a load of beehives to a distant town. Her father should have made the delivery but he had got home too drunk to set out himself. The following passage describes Tess and Abraham talking together as they jog along in the cart:

Abraham talked on, rather for the pleasure of utterance than for audition, so that his sister's abstraction was of no account. He leant back against the hives, and with upturned face made observations on the stars, whose cold pulses were beating amid the black hollows above, in serene dissociation from these two wisps of human life. He asked how far away those twinklers were, and whether God was on the other side of them. But ever and anon his childish prattle recurred to what impressed his imagination even more deeply than the wonders of creation. If Tess were made rich by marrying a gentleman, would she have money enough to buy a spy-glass so large that it would draw the stars as near to her as Nettlecombe-Tout? [Nettlecombe-Tout is a nearby village.]

The renewed subject, which seemed to have impregnated the whole family, filled Tess with impatience.

'Never mind that now!' she exclaimed.

'Did you say the stars were worlds, Tess?'

'Yes.'

'All like ours?'

'I don't know; but I think so. They sometimes seem to be like the apples on our stubbard-tree. Most of them splendid and sound — a few blighted.'

'Which do we live on — a splendid one or a blighted one?'

'A blighted one.'

' 'Tis very unlucky that we didn't pitch on a sound one, when there were so many more of 'em!'

'Yes.'

'Is it like that *really*, Tess?' said Abraham, turning to her much impressed, on reconsideration of this rare information. 'How would it have been if we had pitched on a sound one?'

'Well, father wouldn't have coughed and creeped about as he does, and wouldn't have got too tipsy to go this journey; and mother wouldn't have been always washing and never getting finished.'

'And you would have been a rich lady ready-made, and not have to be made it by marrying a gentleman?'

'O Aby, don't — don't talk of that any more.'

Left to his reflections Abraham soon grew drowsy. . . . [Tess] made him a sort of nest in front of the hives . . . and, taking the reins into her own hands, jogged on as before. . . . With no longer a companion to distract her, Tess fell more deeply into reverie than ever, her back leaning against the hives. The mute procession past her shoulder of trees and hedges became attached to fantastic scenes outside reality, and the occasional heave of the wind became the sigh of some immense sad soul, conterminous with the universe in space, and with history in time.

Then, examining the mesh of events in her own life, she seemed to see the vanity of her father's pride; the gentlemanly suitor awaiting herself in her mother's fancy; to see him as a grimacing personage, laughing at her poverty . . . Everything grew more and more extravagant, and she no longer knew how time passed. A sudden jerk shook her in her seat, and Tess awoke from the sleep into which she, too, had fallen.

. . . The lantern hanging at her waggon had gone out, but another was shining in her face – much brighter than her own had been. Something terrible had happened. The harness was entangled with an object which blocked the way.[7]

This is a much more complex and difficult passage than any of the ones that precede it. Some of the difficulties arise from the occasional abstractness of Hardy's language: 'Abraham talked on – rather for the pleasure of utterance than for audition' means that he enjoyed talking whether or not anyone listened to him. 'The renewed subject, which seemed to have impregnated the whole family, filled Tess with impatience' simply means that Tess was annoyed at being reminded of the fact that every member of her family seemed obsessed with the idea that she would marry a rich man. Some people would say that such phrases are characteristic of Hardy's rather clumsy style. But perhaps we are now able to recognise that there is more than one kind of language in this passage.

There is, of course, the language of Tess and Abraham: it is simple, though it refers to questions which are far from simple in themselves. Like the speech of Jeremy Tugwell, it contains occasional words and phrases which are drawn from peasant life and show that Tess and her brother are simple country people: but they are not represented as stupid or comic. There is no fine gentleman against whom they can be measured. The imagined gentleman (who is supposed to marry Tess) is represented as 'grimacing' and 'laughing at her poverty' – scarcely a sympathetic figure.

The conversation between Tess and Abraham is simply expressed but it concerns matters of profound significance. The starry sky about them is compared to the apples on a common apple-tree. Most of them are healthy, but some are unfit to eat. All the stars, according to Tess, are worlds like our own: but our world is a bad one. Notice the idea Tess has of a good world: in it nothing would go wrong; nobody would be ill or poor or weak or likely to get drunk. Abraham underlines the dream-like quality of Tess's notion of the world by saying, 'And you would have been a rich lady ready-made.' Abraham is too innocent and too fond of his sister to intend any irony here. He simply carries her thinking one step further: but that one further step renders Tess's thinking absurd. The irony is not intended by Abraham: but it is intended by Hardy.

The dialogue between brother and sister is part of the pattern of the novel. The thoughtful narrative which Hardy has written is closely integrated with the simple language he gives to his country folk. Notice how he speaks of the stars before Abraham begins his dialogue with Tess. Their 'pulses' are 'cold' and 'in serene dissociation from these two wisps of human life'. How effective the word 'wisp' is, conveying as it does the short-lived insubstantial quality of human life, especially as contrasted with the immense size and distance and endurance of the stars. Just as human things are closer to the imagination of the young boy than the wonders of the universe, so the universe is apparently indifferent to human life. And yet Tess speaks of the good star as specially designed for human happiness. Hardy, as narrator, makes no comment on the discrepancy between his description of the indifferent stars and Tess's belief that good stars favour humanity. He allows Abraham's innocent remark, that in Tess's world people would be rich by nature, to suggest to the reader that Tess is day-dreaming.

When Abraham falls asleep, Tess continues with her 'reverie'. The trees and hedges become part of her train of thought and Tess transforms the world around her into a model or metaphor for the unhappiness of mankind. As she becomes more and more absorbed in thinking about herself, she falls asleep and is jerked awake by an accident. In fact, what has happened is that the horse she is guiding has been killed by colliding with the mail-cart.

Hardy does not explicitly blame Tess for causing the death of the horse. He sets down her musings about the nature of the world side by side with his own description of it. He allows her fond dreams of the world as it might be to collide with the world as it is. He allows the comment of the child to cast doubt on the opinion Tess has uttered as an older, and presumably wiser, adult. Just as Pip (or the narrator) in the extract from *Great Expectations* used the natural scene as a way of commenting on human experience, so Hardy allows Tess to use it in the same way, but he also reminds us that there is no real natural harmony between them. In Hardy's view the real world is not naturally fitted to the hopes and wishes of human beings.

Very little of the language of *Tess of the d'Urbervilles* is concerned with telling us what happened. The events in Hardy's novels are arranged to display a pattern in human affairs which he offers for our consideration and comment. The events of a novel by Hardy, and the language in which they are narrated, are woven together to form a structure of meanings which goes far beyond anything which can be reduced to 'story' or 'plot'. Only an expanded interpretation can do justice to this pattern of meanings; any attempt to summarise it inevitably reduces its scope and weakens its effect.

New Voices

'. . . Won't it be strange to see fields of snow?' They laughed. Neither of them had ever seen snow. It was to them something heroic, primeval, belonging to the possible antique history of their race; and the icy seas, the fog-bound coasts, the groaning walls of ice, the night-, crime-, and misery-beleaguered island of Great Britain, something that occurred in the legends of Norsemen, something that froze Little Time and that existed also in the black latitudes of dead planets. It was not the dainty snow of Christmas cards that they believed in, broken by tinsel, robins, and ivy, but the icy death of the whale-gate, Ultima Thule. They shrank from the land they were going to, a land of tyranny denounced by English patriots and abandoned by their own grandfathers, a land of unrest, the land of Dickens, poor seamstresses in Poultry and mud-spattered Watling Street, a London, cloud-sunk, an adamantine island chained to the shifting bank of the Channel, the city of Limehouse and Jack the Ripper; and the Alps they saw in imagination were sky-piercing, snow blazing pinnacles, sharp as wolf-teeth, in a pass of which, over-looking a pine forest, a blue-shirted shepherd opened his hairy chest to the *tramontana* and dangled at his belt an unsheathed knife with which he attacked the wolves. At the same instant Hannibal crossed with elephants panting out of wells of snow and a brave little drummer boy drummed from a crevasse; upon the glacier, the ice-maiden beckoned; in an evergreen flow of ice issuing from the side of a precipice a corpse lay for ever fresh. In the forest, long-haired timber-cutters worked, the wolves howled; in short, the land of ice-Cockaigne, without time or race. Their land of the sun seemed to them a sparkling land, set in blue seas, and much preferable, but they had to go, called out by the sea, driven forth on its ships, they could not stay in the busy port of Sydney and not take all the chances it offered of distant seas.[8]

The voice here is that of the narrator of *For Love Alone* (1945) by Christina Stead (1902–   ), who was born in Australia, though she lived for a long time in the United States of America. Here her heroine and the man she is to accompany to England share their thoughts about what the experience might be like. Their expectations are almost entirely drawn from literature: they have read of the heroic exploits of the Norse invaders who crossed dangerous seas to invade Europe in the ninth and tenth centuries, so their idea of snow is not confined to the pretty illustration of Victorian Christmas cards. In contrast to the light and warmth of Australia, England seems forbidding, harsh, unjust and frightening, though their idea of Europe, equally based on fairy-story and legend, seems heroic, romantic, enchanted, inviting. But they know that their fantasies are false (Cockaigne was a legendary country described in mediaeval tales), though they cannot resist the attraction of distant places, so rich in legend and history. In their imaginations the picture of the hardy Swiss shepherd, shirt open to the cold of the North wind, mingles with a memory of the exploits of the Carthaginian general Hannibal (247BC–183BC) who used elephants to help his army to invade Italy by crossing the Alps.

This voice is earnest, learned, imaginative, but perhaps a little naive. Christina Stead wants to convey to her readers a sense of the immaturity of her character, while impressing upon us her intelligence and appetite for books. Contrast this with a quite different, more modern voice:

The place where Tolroy and the family living was off the Harrow Road, and the people in that area call the Working Class. Wherever in London that it have Working Class, there you will find a lot of spades. This is the real world, where men know what it is to hustle a pound to pay the rent when Friday come. The houses around here old and grey and weatherbeaten, the walls cracking like the last days of Pompeii, it ain't have no hot water, and in the whole street that Tolroy and them living in, none of the houses have bath. You had was to buy one of them big galvanise basin and boil the water and full it up, or else go to the public bath. Some of the houses still had gas light, which is to tell you how old they was. All the houses in a row in the street, on both sides, they build like one long house with walls separating them in parts, so your house jam-up between two neighbours: is so most of the houses is in London. The street does be always dirty except if rain fall. Sometimes a truck does

come with a kind of revolving broom and some pipes letting out
water, and the driver drive near the pavement, and water come out
the pipes and the broom revolve, and so they sweep the road. It
always have little children playing in the road, because they ain't
have no other place to play. They does draw hopscotch blocks on
the pavement, and other things, and some of the walls of the
building have signs painted like Vote Labour and Down with the
Tories. The bottom of the street, it had a sweet-shop, a bakery,
a grocery, a butcher and a fish and chips. The top of the street,
where it join the Harrow Road, it had all kind of thing – shop, store,
butcher, green-grocer, trolley and bus stop. Up here on a Saturday
plenty vendors used to be selling provisions near the pavements. It
had a truck used to come one time with flowers to sell, and the
fellars used to sell cheap, and the poor people buy tulip and daffodil
to put in the dingy room they living in.[9]

To some, this voice – that of Samuel Selvon (1927–   ) in *The Lonely
Londoners* (1956) – might appear somewhat shocking. Are there some
misprints, it might be asked? On closer inspection the English is
perfectly intelligible and consistent by its own standards. 'There is'
has been replaced by 'it have', 'you must' by 'you had was': some
verbs and verb endings have been dropped. This is a written form of
the English of Trinidad: apart from the grammatical differences,
however, the language Selvon uses has an attractive clarity as well as
the strong rhythms of literary English prose. Of course it is constructed
on a deliberately simple model; look carefully at the following
sentence:

> Sometimes a truck does come with a kind of revolving broom and
> some pipes letting out water, and the driver drive near the pavement,
> and water come out the pipes and the broom revolve, and so they
> sweep the road.

Perhaps it reminds us a bit of those sentences quoted in an earlier
chapter from the Anglo-Saxon Chronicle: each element of the sentence
is linked simply by 'and'. If you look at the rest of the paragraph, you
will see that this is true of most of the other sentences. And yet the
paragraph does not simply describe the London in which Tolroy and
his family live; it also offers a judgement. It accepts in the most
straightforward way the dirt, the deprivation, the cramped and restric-

ted living space, the sharp class divisions of the city. The final statement
of the paragraph — 'and the poor people buy tulip and daffodil to put
in the dingy room they living in' — sets against the physical squalor it
describes the sense of beauty, the determination not to be quenched by
the environment, which is a feature of the novel as a whole.

This voice may appear simple, but the simplicity is deceptive. The
paragraph as a whole has a unity and a control which suggests a
sophisticated literary intention: notice how it moves between the
bottom and the top of the street which joins the Harrow Road. The
writer's attention moves from the squalor of the bottom end to the
comparative affluence and excitement of the Harrow Road. There is
some promise, some object to aim at. The bottom of the street has the
bare necessities of life, perhaps, but the top of the street offers a
glimpse of wider horizons which are there to be explored. The
organisation of the paragraph is not elaborate, but it is consciously
ordered. And it is this sense of ordered arrangement which confirms
our initial impression of the aesthetic distinction of the writing despite
the unfamiliar linguistic forms in which it is conveyed.

A third voice — from *The Beautyful Ones are Not Yet Born* (1969)
by Ayi Kwei Armah — sounds a very different note. Armah's novel is
about the corruption that can accompany power. It is about the
temptations which may be offered to politicians and the sense of
estrangement which a man may feel from a society which too readily
accepts injustice. Armah's voice is harsh and accusatory, but impressive.
The first extract starkly describes the situation which the protagonist of
the novel — simply called 'the man' — finds himself in:

'If you want to talk to someone higher up . . .'
'My friend,' the visitor said, 'don't joke with me. I need to talk
to you.'
'I tell you I have nothing to do with bookings.'
'You can see that clerk for me.' The visitor looked suspiciously
towards the door, then plunged his left arm underneath his *kente*
folds. When the arm emerged it was clutching a dark brown leather
wallet. The wallet was not fat. The man looked steadily at the
visitor. The visitor's gaze was bent, his eyes looking in the wallet
while thick fingers fumbled inside. Then the fingers brought out two
carefully held-out notes, two green tens. The man said nothing.
The visitor put the ten-cedi notes under a stone paperweight on the
table behind the man, to his right. The visitor drew his hand back

from the table and the notes and stood staring at the man in front of him. The man said nothing.

'Take it,' the visitor said. 'One for you, one for him.'

'Why should I?'

The look on the visitor's face made it plain that to this kind of question no sane man would give an answer. But then suddenly the visitor's expression changed, and he laughed a laugh that came out too high, like a woman's or a child's. 'You are a funny man, you this man,' he said. 'You think I am a fool to be giving you just ten cedis?' Again the high laugh. 'Is nothing. I know ten is nothing. So, my friend, what do you drink?'

The man looked levelly at the visitor and gave his answer. 'Water.'[10]

This prose draws no attention to itself. It is as clear as the water which signifies the man's integrity. Armah is so interested in his subject matter that he makes every effort to make his prose a translucent vehicle for the scene he wishes to set before the reader's imagination. The sentences are simple in syntax as well as in vocabulary. Each sentence is a codification of a single significant action. Only occasionally does the narrator intervene to comment on the action: when he tells us, 'The look on the visitor's face made it plain that to this kind of question no sane man would give an answer', the narrator acts as an interpreter between the reader, the man who is offering the bribe and the man who is behaving in such an eccentric way that he appears to be insane. What the comment makes clear is that both men are acting in good faith, although the conventions to which they adhere are incompatible. The man who offers the money is obeying a set of social rules which are repugnant to the man who refuses. We can understand his anger and frustration, although it is clear that the author's sympathy is not in his favour.

Elsewhere in the novel Armah speaks directly to the reader about his disappointment and anger that political independence has not brought freedom from human weakness. His novel is fiercely didactic. The title of the book reflects his idealistic hope that human beings may one day appear who have shed their inborn egotism. Sometimes he dramatises his feeling as in the following passage where 'the man' has a dream:

Blinding lights, wild and uncontrolled, succeeded by pure darkness, from which the recognised self emerges. The man sees himself, very small, very sharp, very clear. Walking with an unknown companion, scarcely ever seen, in the coolness of some sweet dusk, leaving the dark low hovels behind. Out in the distance, far away but very clearly visible, a group of shining white towers, having the stamp of the university tower at Legon and the sheer white side of the Atlantic-Caprice. They are going there, the two of them, the man and his companion, happy in the present and happy in the image of the future in the present.

But brutal lights shine and cut into the night with their sudden power, rushing with their harsh rhythm towards the happy pair, now so confused. The lights move forward, smooth and powerful. The man, blinded by a cutting beam, covers his downcast eyes with his hands, and in the movement lets go of his companion's waist. But she is not blinded. Through the insufficient protection of his fingers he can see her, her eyes shining with the potent brightness of huge car lights; returning the power of the oncoming lights. They come, the lights, with the noise of the cars bringing them. Sound, hardly audible, of a new door opening. Floating upward in the air, the man's companion lands inside the car in the lead. The other cars . . . swing up behind the first, and all of them go off in the direction of the towers, leaving the man behind. The white towers gleam with a supernatural radiance as the cars get closer to them, then everything penetrates slowly, smoothly into darkness as they enter. Every shining thing goes out when only the man is left, and the darkness turns keenly cold. Looking for warmth, he lies down, but the ground is also cold and very hard. The man tries to find his way back into the old warmth of the hovels he has left behind, but looking back, he finds he can never again know the way back there. All he can feel now is the cold, and a loneliness that corrodes his heart with its despair, with the knowledge that he has lost his happy companion forever, and he cannot ever live alone.[11]

Even here, in the dream, Armah's writing is strongly didactic. The dream has some of the quality of allegory which Bunyan used to such effect in *Pilgrim's Progress*. The man and woman in the dream stand for contemporary men and women in a precisely indicated space–time, but isolated, in darkness, on the road, linked by the man's arm round the woman's waist they remind us of an aboriginal human pair, Adam and Eve, awakening simultaneously to a knowledge of themselves and to a knowledge of the tempting evil of power. The woman, like Eve, more readily succumbs to its promise of an easy life. The man, left behind, realises he cannot return to an innocence which has been destroyed forever. Armah's language does not lose its effective simplicity here; the disconnected images with which the dream begins are expressed in sharply visualised verbless phrases. The initial disruption, which brings the man to a sense of self-consciousness, is superseded by the glowing lights which are metaphors for a new social order based on power, affluence and the products of technological change. The man is blinded; the woman's eyes are opened. By employing in this way the old technique of dream-allegory, Armah clearly demonstrates that it has not lost its rhetorical power to clarify by simplification complex social and moral issues.

These examples can only indicate some of the new directions taken by fiction written in English. A separate volume would be needed to study their range and diversity. What is more relevant for the purpose of this book is to notice continuities within change. These new voices have extended the traditions from which they draw their sense of aesthetic form, but in doing so they demonstrate the strength and coherence of the tradition.

4 *How the Story Gets Told*

Episode and Plot

When we considered (in Chapter 2) some of the ways of telling a story – some of the elements of fiction – we noticed that histories might be divided into two types: one of them we might call the 'and then' type, the other, the 'because' type. The first had no special interest in considering what linked the events it recounted; it offered no explanation for them in terms of circumstance, or environment, or in terms of the character and past history of the people who took part in them. The second was keenly interested in tracing a causal pattern in the events which were described; it looked at behaviour, and at its causes and motivation; it was interested in details because it searched for the causes of behaviour in the minute particulars of human action.

This distinction between the chronicle – the 'and then' type – and the analytical history – the 'because' type – can usefully be applied to novels. 'What happened next?' is a question we all like to ask; Queen Scheherezade in *The Arabian Nights* saved her life by always having a new story to tell. The 'romances' – long tales of heroic adventure – were fictions of the 'and then' type. The kind of novels which were written during the nineteenth century in Britain, France, Russia and the United States were mainly 'because' novels. Novelists were increasingly interested in demonstrating connections – in showing the links between events, or between people and their environment, or in making grander analyses of the nature and destiny of human beings. Novels of this kind not only analysed how people had behaved, they made recommendations about how people might or should behave. The novelist was not just a teller of tales; he was a philosopher, moralist, theologian, preacher and prophet.

When novels become ways of looking at the world something odd happens to how their stories get told. A sequence of events, however strange or exciting, has no explanatory power. The world is too complex to be described in a straightforward way: the linear sequence of events in time does not provide an adequate model for their convoluted and subtle interrelationships. It would be an over-simplification to say that the history of the novel shows an unbroken development from 'and then' types to 'because' types. Contemporary novelists seem to have given up hope of representing the world by dense, complex, coherent fictions. But perhaps it is at least roughly true to say that the novel has developed from being a loose collection of episodes, where almost anything could find a place, to a much more carefully organised composition, in which every detail was indispensable and every feature of its composition was governed by a central design.

A straightforward example of the first type of novel we have been discussing is the anonymously written *Lazarillo de Tormes*, published in Spanish in 1554, in which the central character, Lazaro, recounts his adventures from birth to marriage in a succession of chapters which tell how he passed through the hands of various masters, from blind beggar to priest to penniless grandee, and from a friar whose vices are too scandalous to be named to a seller of indulgences. All Lazaro's masters are cruel or mean or penniless; the tale abounds in violence and trickery. Its aim is to expose the vices of the world through a number of representative figures, and to show what kind of wits, unscrupulously used, are needed to survive in it. Lazaro prides himself on having to look after himself in a hard world. Since he ends up as a town-crier, married to a woman whose virtue is not beyond reproach, it is not clear whether his career is to be rated a success or a failure. At least he has moved from total poverty, which forces him to live by his wits, to a modestly comfortable existence with which he claims to be happy.

Lazarillo de Tormes was a model for many subsequent novels, usually known as 'picaresque' novels, because they were stories about 'picaros', rogues who had learned enough tricks to look after themselves. Because they look at society from the point of view of the sharp-witted rogue, they are usually satirical. 'Picaresque' novels have these two features: they are episodic since the adventures of the rogue may be added to at will by the author, but they tend to expose rascality and cunning because their episodes are linked by a central character whose capacity for getting into trouble is only equalled by his ability for getting out of it. Clearly, then, even the most episodic novel may be developed in a consistent direction. As episode follows episode, the reader discovers with the picaro that roguery is to be found everywhere, even in the highest places. What began as a string of adventures becomes a stinging satire on society.

Lazarillo de Tormes is a short book of seven chapters; *Gil Blas*, a novel of the same kind, set in Spain though written by a Frenchman, Alain-René Lesage (1668–1747), consists of twelve books in which are recorded the adventures of its hero, Gil Blas, as he moves through the ranks of Spanish society from a robbers' cave to the court of the king of Spain. Embedded in his story, however, are the more briefly recounted lives and adventures of many of the people he meets on the way.

Gil Blas's own taste in story-telling is akin to the material in Lesage's novel: when asked by one of his servants whether he would like him to 'go through all the fabulous histories of wandering knights, distressed damsels, giants, enchanted castles, and the whole train of legendary adventures', he replies, 'I had much rather hear your own true history.' The true histories recounted in *Gil Blas* may sometimes strain the reader's belief, but it is for their closeness to the detailed circumstances of everyday life that they were valued. Lesage's narratives may lack psychological subtlety, but they are packed with incident. Many English novels, such as those of Tobias Smollett (1721–71) were written in the tradition of the picaresque novel, as were the early novels of Charles Dickens (1812–70) such as *Pickwick Papers* (1837) and *Nicholas Nickleby* (1839). Modern novels such as *The Confessions of Felix Krull, Confidence Man* (1954) by Thomas Mann (1875–1955) and *The Adventures of Augie March* (1953) by Saul Bellow (1915–   ) show that the tradition is still alive.

During the lifetime – and within the practice – of the greatest English novelist of the nineteenth century, Charles Dickens, writers began to pay far closer attention to the organisation of their novels: gradually it came to be assumed that there should be some principles of growth in the novel so that each part was integrally related to the whole. A novel such as Dickens's *Little Dorrit* (1857) is designed to show how the widely different groups and individuals who crowd its scenes are in fact closely related to one another and belong to a society which, for all its diversity, faces a common destiny. As we read it, the novel moves them irresistibly closer to one another, so that we can almost feel the strength of the current of narrative which draws the characters together. In such a novel, each part grows out of what has gone before: expectations are aroused in the reader that are satisfied or confounded by events which, at least in retrospect, can be seen to be coherent. In the later nineteenth and early twentieth centuries a unified method of construction was most highly regarded. In a series of Prefaces to the collected edition of his novels, Henry James (1843–1916) laid the foundations of a theory of the novel which admirers treated as if it were orthodox belief. Systematising critics fixed his methods into what might almost be called rules by which a good novel might be recognised.

One of the principal criteria for success was that the action of the novel should be coherent and unified. If we call to mind the action of *Pride and Prejudice* we will remember that it consists of a number of strands: we can think of each of the girls in the novel as contributing a strand to the bundle of stories which makes up the narrative. They are unified because each of them is seen in the light of the theme of marriage (or marriageability). At the centre of the novel is the complicated story of Elizabeth Bennet and Darcy, which after many confusions successfully ends in marriage. During the course of the novel suggestions are made about what constitutes a successful marriage, and the stories of the other girls are contrasted with Elizabeth's to sketch out less successful marriages, or in the case of Jane Bennet and Bingley, success of a different kind, or in the case of Mary the total failure of the dully unmarriageable. The satisfaction of reading a novel of this kind is that the course of its action presents us with a dramatised argument. Jane Austen does not tell us what to think about her characters or how to go about choosing partners for life. But by demonstrating the consequences of different ways of behaving, she makes us think more deeply about the issues involved.

If unity is thought to be a desirable quality in a novel, some limitation must be put on the novelist's material. Jane Austen made a famous remark to the effect that five families in a village was just the kind of material she liked to work on. But even such a small group could provide material for many volumes. Simply to limit the number of characters does not itself produce unity.

Point of View

One of the methods which have been suggested to increased the unity of a novel is to pay close attention to what has been called 'point of view'. In its technical sense, this phrase means 'the angle from which a fictional work is narrated'. Many novels have been narrated by an author who knows everything about his characters and who is able to follow processes of thought normally hidden from everyone except the thinker. It is commonplace nowadays that some of these processes may even be hidden from the conscious mind of the agent or character whose behaviour is being described. Is there perhaps a danger that a novelist might be discredited if he seemed to know too much about his characters? If we find tales of witches, of wizards or flying carpets unbelievable, why should we believe an author who tells us what his characters are thinking?

The author who knows everything is commonly called 'the omniscient author'. He tells his story in the third person; he has by convention a privileged access into the thoughts and intentions of his characters; he may also enter into the story in person to talk to the reader or to comment on what his characters are doing. If there is a danger that such an all-knowing author may not be believed, there is equally a danger that he may get in the way of the story. Authors who intrude to comment on their characters may simply annoy the reader in the end. A further objection to the method of omniscient narration is that the action and the characters are likely to be too far away from the reader. Where everything must be seen through the eyes of the author, there is a danger that we shall be told everything in summary form, whereas what the reader wants is an uninterrupted close-up view of the scene. To tell the reader what is happening, rather than to show him, is the persistent vice of this kind of story-telling.

One method of restricting the scope of the narrator and of providing greater conciseness is to confine the narrative to the thoughts and experience of one character. In *Pride and Prejudice* Jane Austen is able to move from an unrestricted omniscient point of view to a much more narrowly focused narrative which, without departing from the third person, selects Elizabeth Bennet as a centre from whose angle of vision the characters and action are seen. It is possible for an author to make further refinements of this technique so that all the events and actions of the novel are presented through the consciousness of one central character. If the author presents what the character remembers as well as what he sees or hears or smells in the random order in which these experiences may occur, he is using the technique of 'stream of consciousness'. Here, for example, is the central character of *Ulysses* by James Joyce (1882–1941) making breakfast for his wife:

Another slice of bread and butter: three, four; right. She didn't
like her plate full. Right. He turned from the tray, lifted the kettle
off the hob and set it sideways on the fire. It sat there, dull and
squat, its spout stuck out. Cup of tea soon. Good. Mouth dry. The
cat walked stiffly round a leg of the table with tail on high.
— Mkgnao!
— O, there you are, Mr. Bloom said, turning from the fire. The cat
mewed in answer and stalked again stiffly round a leg of the table,
mewing. Just how she stalks over my writingtable. Prr. Scratch my
head. Prr.

    Mr. Bloom watched curiously, kindly, the lithe black form. Clean
to see: the gloss of her sleek hide, the white button under the butt
of her tail, the green flashing eyes. He bent down to her, his hands
on his knees.
— Milk for the pussens, he said.
— Mrkgnao! the cat cried.[1]

Although there is narrative here, and some authorial judgements —
'curiously, kindly' are inferences about Mr Bloom's behaviour from the
point of view of an outside observer — the prose slides into a truncated
version of what Mr Bloom might be saying to himself. Mr Bloom's
thought processes are a kind of primitive inner speech, which the
narrator can infer, in much the same way as Mr Bloom himself
translates the cat's mewing into commands. Although Joyce's
procedure may seem unfamiliar at first, it is not essentially different
from the movement back and forward (in Jane Austen) from
omniscient narrator to limited point of view. It might be a good
exercise to look carefully at each sentence and trace it to its source in
the narrator or in Mr Bloom's thought or speech. How has Joyce
managed to eliminate the narrator from the scene and concentrate
wholly on Bloom? On second thoughts, *has* he quite eliminated the
narrator?
    A further example of a strictly limited point of view, which does not
attempt to enter into the thought processes of the character in such a
direct way, comes from the opening paragraph of *The Wings of the
Dove* (1902) by Henry James:

She waited, Kate Croy, for her father to come in, but he kept her
unconscionably, and there were moments at which she showed
herself, in the glass over the mantel, a face positively pale with the

irritation that had brought her to the point of going away without
sight of him. It was at this point, however, that she remained;
changing her place, moving from the shabby sofa to the armchair
upholstered in a glazed cloth that gave at once — she had tried it —
the sense of the slippery and the sticky. She had looked at the
sallow prints on the walls and at the lovely magazine, a year old, that
combined, with a small lamp in coloured glass and a knitted white
centre-piece wanting in freshness, to enhance the effect of the
purplish cloth on the principal table; she had above all, from time to
time, taken a brief stand on the small balcony to which the pair of
long windows gave access. The vulgar little street, in this view,
offered scant relief from the vulgar little room; its main office was
to suggest to her that the narrow black house-fronts, adjusted to
a standard that would have been low even for backs, constituted
quite the publicity implied by such privacies. One felt them in the
room exactly as one felt the room — the hundred like it, or worse —
in the street. Each time she turned in again, each time, in her
impatience, she gave him up, it was to sound to a deeper depth,
while she tasted the faint, flat emanation of things, the failure of
fortune and of honour. If she continued to wait it was really, in a
manner, that she might not add the shame of fear, of individual,
personal collapse, to all the other shames. To feel the street, to feel
the room, to feel the table-cloth and the centre-piece and the lamp,
gave her a small, salutary sense at least of neither shirking nor lying.
This whole vision was the worst thing yet — as including, in
particular, the interview for which she had prepared herself; and for
what had she come for but for the worst? She tried to be sad, so as
not to be angry; but it made her angry that she couldn't be sad. And
yet where was misery, misery too beaten for blame and chalk-
marked by fate like a 'lot' at a common auction, if not in these
merciless signs of mere mean, stale feelings.[2]

That is probably the most complex and difficult piece of prose that
you will be asked to read in this book. Some of the difficulty arises
from the fact that James constantly adds qualifications to his sentences
so that the reader's attention is diverted from the core of meaning of
the sentence; sometimes pronouns are not quite clearly related to the
words for which they stand. In the sentence 'one felt them in the room
exactly as one felt the room . . . in the street' it is necessary to know
that 'them' refers to 'the narrow black house-fronts' in the previous

sentence. A good example of James's hesitation – his deliberate with-holding of the sense of the sentence – occurs in the following: 'Each time she turned in again [from the balcony, that is], each time, in her impatience, she gave him up, it was to sound to a deeper depth, while she tasted the faint, flat emanation of things, the failure of fortune and honour.' Kate Croy is caught between the outside and the inside of the mean room in her father's house which so distresses her. The street and the room seem to mirror one another. As she turns back into the room, thinking her father is not coming, she catches once again its stale atmosphere which suggests to her the fact of her father's failure. Everything which happens in this paragraph is recorded as it affects Kate's senses and passes into her understanding. By using the phrase 'it was to sound to a deeper depth', James prepares us for Kate's insightful grasp of her father's situation, but what she grasps – 'the failure of fortune and honour' – is based on a direct sensation – on the taste of the 'faint, flat emanation of things'. (How well he captures that mingling of the sense of taste and smell which comes to us from a badly ventilated room.) In the same way – through Kate Croy – we know that the armchair is 'slippery and sticky' because she has touched it. If James wants us to have some glimpse of her mood, he shows her aware-ness of herself as she glances in the mirror. In contrast with Joyce's portrayal of Mr Bloom, there is nothing random in James's presentation of Kate Croy's thoughts and sensations. The paragraph carries with it an argument; implicitly it has the form of a question and answer. Why did Kate Croy not leave this dreary room where her father was keeping her waiting? Because she wanted to appreciate to the full the horrors of a life of poverty which angered her, and which she had not yet decided to reject. She wanted to see clearly the meanness which her father's house appeared to represent; she wanted to know the worst.

But look carefully at that last rhetorical question in the paragraph which seems to expect no answer. It is clearly obvious to Kate Croy that her father's house represents meanness and misery. But James has so written the sentence that the reader may detect in Kate's own response – in particular in her inability to be sympathetically sad – the merciless sign of mere mean feeling, which she attributes to her surroundings.

Such a technique is satisfyingly resourceful: we see the situation from the principal character's point of view, but there is also an oblique hint that another view is possible. We are able to share Kate Croy's vision of things, even if we are not invited to accept her at her own

valuation. In her novel *Mansfield Park* (1814) Jane Austen describes a
very similar scene where Fanny Price, her heroine, returns to the
poorish home from which she has been removed to be brought up
among much richer cousins. Here is Jane Austen's account of what
Fanny finds when she returns home after many years' absence:

> It was the abode of noise, disorder, and impropriety. Nobody was
> in their right place, nothing was done as it ought to be. She could
> not respect her parents, as she had hoped. On her father, her confi-
> dence had not been sanguine but he was more negligent of his
> family, his habits were worse and his manners coarser, than she had
> been prepared for. . . . Her disappointment in her mother was
> greater; *there* she had hoped much, and found almost nothing. Every
> flattering scheme of being of consequence to her soon fell to the
> ground. Mrs. Price was not unkind — but, instead of gaining on her
> affection and confidence, and becoming more and more dear, her
> daughter never met with greater kindness from her, than on the first
> day of her arrival. The instinct of nature was soon satisfied, and
> Mrs. Price's attachment had no other source. . . .
>
> Much of all this, Fanny could not but be sensible of. She might
> scruple to make use of the words, but she must and did feel that her
> mother was a partial, ill-judging parent, a dawdle, a slattern, who
> neither taught nor restrained her children, whose house was the
> scene of mismanagement and discomfort from beginning to end, and
> who had no talent, no conversation, no affection towards herself;
> no curiosity to know her better, no desire of her friendship, and no
> inclination for her company that could lessen her sense of such
> feelings.[3]

These two examples, from Henry James and Jane Austen, neatly
illustrate the fineness of the distinction between the omniscient and the
limited point of view. The first paragraph of the second extract is
written in words that we might imagine to have gone through the mind
of Fanny Price. If it were re-written in the first person rather than the
third person, there is no awkward authorial intrusion which would
need to be removed. It would be too much to say that Fanny's response
to her parents is shown from her point of view, but it is written as a
close summary of what her feelings must have been: Henry James, on
the other hand, is careful to place every sight and sensation in the
consciousness of Kate Croy. Jane Austen summarises; she does not

show us, as Henry James does, the interpenetration of thought and sensation, or the crystallisation of perceptions into thoughts.

It takes longer for the reader to follow Kate Croy's train of thought, because we watch it forming as she moves restlessly about the room slowly coming to see clearly why she is there and what she is waiting for. By contrast Jane Austen provides a fluent series of firmly articulated judgements. In the second paragraph of the extract from *Mansfield Park* the narrator's presence is inescapable. She is able to utter the unequivocal sentiments about her heroine's mother which Fanny Price might have felt but might have been unable to put into words. 'A partial, ill-judging parent, a dawdle, a slattern, who neither taught nor restrained her children' — the judgement is the narrator's, but it arises incontestably from the feelings and perceptions she has allowed her character to experience.

The difference in the narrative techniques of Jane Austen and Henry James can be summed up thus: Jane Austen *tells* us what her character is thinking, Henry James *shows* us. That the novelist should retire from the scene and render his story-telling as dramatically as he could was a further element in the theory of fiction associated with the practice of Henry James. In *Mansfield Park* the narrator follows the action as if she were a historian; in *The Wings of the Dove* he accompanies it as if he were a dramatist, or even a film-maker, recording the action, outer and inner, as it occurs. In *Mansfield Park* the narrator makes explicit the judgements which seem appropriate about the behaviour of the characters which has been described; in *The Wings of the Dove* there is room for doubt about how the character is to be judged. The narrator does not relieve the reader of the responsibility for coming to a conclusion. We see everything from Kate Croy's point of view, but we are still looking at her behaviour from the outside; we may follow and understand what she thinks and how she behaves, but we are still bound to decide whether or not to approve of her behaviour.

'First Person' Narrative

If the narrator tells the story in the first person, the author is no longer able to intervene in the story directly. A narrator, who is a witness to the events of the novel, has no special access to the minds of the other characters involved. *Lord Jim* (1900) by Joseph Conrad

(1857–1924) is a novel which begins in the third person, told by an impersonal omniscient narrator. After the fourth chapter, the novel is handed over to a first-person narrator who then relates the rest of the novel from this point of view. Conrad then allows his narrator, Marlow, to intrude into the story he is telling: he enters into dialogue, not directly with the reader, but indirectly through a circle of friends supposed to be listening to his tale, since Marlow is represented as spinning a yarn to his sailor friends after a good dinner. He is permitted the ruminations, the digressions, the abrupt switch of emphasis and mood of a story-teller speaking aloud in a diffuse conversational style. But Marlow is not allowed privileged access into the mind of the man who is the principal character of the book. Just why Jim acted as he did, when he jumped overboard from a passenger-laden ship which he thought was sinking, is the subject of the novel.

The narrator, of course, may be the principal character in the novel, and may take part in the action. Pip in Dickens's *Great Expectations* (1861) is a narrator of this kind. It is his business to relate the events of his life as he looks back upon them. Clearly such a narrator could simply tell us what happened because he knows what has taken place. Dickens does not allow Pip to do this. He makes Pip dramatise his story; his life is presented as if it is as yet unlived. There is no question of omniscience because much of Pip's life is shrouded in mystery from him. He is represented as not knowing, in particular, who is responsible for the money which has transformed him from a blacksmith's apprentice to a 'gentleman', who has prospects which are still to be revealed to him. As has been said, there is a paradox here: Pip is writing long after the events have taken place, so that he is looking back on them with full knowledge of what took place. And yet Dickens places his narrator so that he moves through the story as if he had no idea of what is to come. He has one role as narrator, and another as agent. Dickens does allow Pip one element of hindsight: he is able to comment to some extent on his ingratitude to, and neglect of, the blacksmith, Joe Gargery, who has been the prop and sustainer of his boyhood self, and of Biddy, the girl who befriended him as a youngster and whose affection has never wavered, though it has never been properly appreciated.

As a narrator Pip has a complex role: he is able to look back from a distance on the events of his childhood; he is also able to move close to the action and to report it as if it were happening to him now. In the second chapter of the novel, Pip, close to the action, is able to refer to what is happening 'tonight'. A few pages later he is the much older commentator who is able to say:

> Since that time, which is far enough away now, I have often thought that few people know what secrecy there is in the young, under terror. No matter how unreasonable the terror, so that it be terror. I was in mortal terror of my interlocutor with the ironed leg; I was in mortal terror of myself, from whom an awful promise had been extracted; I had no hope of deliverance through my all-powerful sister, who repulsed me at every turn . . . .[4]

But in the next chapter we are once more looking through the eyes, not of the mature man, but of the young boy who is experiencing his adventures with all the vividness of their occurrence:

> It was a rimy morning, and very damp. I had seen the damp lying on the outside of my little window, as if some goblins had been crying there all night, and using the window for a pocket-handkerchief. Now, I saw the damp lying on the bare hedges and spare grass, like a coarser sort of spiders' webs; hanging itself from twig to twig and blade to blade. On every rail and gate, wet lay clammy; and the marsh-mist was so thick, that the wooden finger on the post directing people to our village . . . was invisible to me until I was quite close under it.[5]

The complexity of the narrator's role in *Great Expectations* must lead us to conclude that it may not be useful merely to label the point of view from which the story is told. Each novel will have features which give the narration a character of its own. The author is writing a novel which must stand on its own independent of himself. He may use many means to fashion his work into a satisfactory whole; 'point of view' is one of those means, but it is only one of a complex set of methods of fictional presentation. Summary, the dramatic presentation of scene, 'point of view', recurrent patterns of imagery, symbolism, the division of the text into books and chapters are only some of the ways of giving shape to fiction, some of which will be examined more carefully later. Even if the author remains aloof from his work and makes no direct contact with the reader, all the choices of methods of presentation are his. His hand is everywhere in the fashioning of the novel, however carefully he may try to conceal it. Even when he does appear in person, it is well to remember that his appearance is carefully tailored to suit the particular purposes of the book. We can make a distinction between the writer of the novel and the authorial presence which appears in the novel. We can sometimes make a distinction between the authorial presence and the voice of the narrator: in *As I Lay Dying* (1930), William Faulkner uses fifteen narrative voices, but they have been made coherent by the shaping spirit of the author. In some novels it is part of the author's design that we should doubt or question the accuracy or the value judgements of the narrator.

The Author's 'Tone of Voice'

No matter from what point of view the narrative has been written, there is likely to be in a novel worth close attention a distinctive tone of voice. Whether a novel is written in the first or the third person, the kind of language its author uses, his attitude to his subject matter and to the reader create very different styles of narrative. In illustrating these differences, we return to the question of the omniscient narrator: let us look at three novels where the authorial presence is particularly noticeable. The narrative voice of the novel addresses the reader in the third person; its owner – some embodiment of the author – knows everything about the events of the novel and much about what happens in the minds of the characters. The narrative voice makes what comments it pleases and has its own attitude to the reader as well as to the events of the novel. But despite these similarities the tone of voice of each narrator is strikingly different.

The first of our three, from *Tom Jones* (1749) by Henry Fielding (1707–54), is describing the differences in character between Squire Western (the father of Fielding's heroine, Sophia) and his sister (here called Mrs Western):

> No two things could be more reverse of each other than were the brother and sister, in most instances; particularly in this, that as the brother never foresaw anything at a distance, but was most sagacious in immediately seeing everything the moment it had happened; so the sister eternally foresaw at a distance, but was not so quick-

sighted to objects before her eyes. Of both these the reader may have observed examples: and, indeed, both their several talents were excessive: for as the sister often foresaw what never came to pass, so the brother often saw much more than was actually the truth.

This was not however the case at present. The same report was brought from the garden, as before had been brought from the chamber, that Madam Sophia was not to be found.

The squire himself now sallied forth, and began to roar forth the name of Sophia as loudly, and in as hoarse a voice, as whileom did Hercules that of Hylas: and as the poet tells us, that the whole shore echoed back the name of that beautiful youth; so did the house, the garden, and all the neighbouring fields, resound nothing but the name of Sophia, in the hoarse voices of men, and in the shrill pipes of women; while Echo seemed so pleased to repeat the beloved sound, that if there is really such a person, I believe Ovid hath belied her sex.

Nothing reigned for a long time but confusion; 'till at last the squire having sufficiently spent his breath, returned to the parlour, where he found Mrs Western and Mr Blifil and threw himself with the utmost dejection of his countenance, into a great chair.[6]

The way in which this prose is written gives it a distinctive quality, which resembles the individual quality of a speaking voice. We might call this quality *tone*, or refer to the *voice* of the author. No matter how much the writer may adopt the speech habits appropriate to his characters; no matter how much we may distinguish the narrator of the tale from the author himself, it is likely that something of the author's presence will be revealed in the choices of language he has made in writing his novel.

The narrative voice of *Tom Jones*, as it is revealed in this fragment of the novel, suggests a witty superiority of the narrator to his material. Brother and sister are sharply contrasted according to two related qualities with the effect of making them slightly ridiculous. That they each have these qualities in excess adds to the impression that the narrator is making a caricature of Squire Western and his sister. When the squire is described as 'sallying forth' and 'roaring' out the name of his daughter, we are inclined to see him as a figure of fun.

The narrative voice, in contrast to the excessive noise and bustle it describes, is cool and carefully controlled. The sentences it produces are elegantly balanced – 'seeing' is differentiated from 'foreseeing', 'garden' opposes 'chamber', 'hoarse voices of the men' is contrasted with 'shrill pipes of the women'. This frantic search for a lost girl is so carefully choreographed by the story-teller that we have no sense of fear for her safety. The classical allusions, which the narrator shares with his reader, imply the broad literary perspective within which the novel is set. For a moment the narrative suspends the bustle of the search so that we can listen to the name of the heroine being echoed and re-echoed by the searchers. And then we are back to reality − to a worried, but comic, father and to a narrator whose ironic mockery of him coexists with sympathy for his genuine concern.

Consider, in contrast, the narrative voice of a passage from *Old Mortality* (1816) by Sir Walter Scott (1771−1832), which describes the route taken by a party of soldiers as they leave a civilised corner of Scotland for a more remote moorland area:

> They had now for more than a mile got free of the woodlands, whose broken glades had, for some time, accompanied them after they had left the woods of Tillitudlem. A few birches and oaks still feathered the narrow ravines, or occupied in dwarf-clusters the hollow plains of the moor. But these were gradually disappearing; and a wide and waste country lay before them, swelling into bare hills of dark heath, intersected by deep gullies; being the passages by which torrents forced their course in winter, and during summer the disproportioned channels for diminutive rivulets that winded their puny way among heaps of stones and gravel, the effects and tokens of their winter fury. This desolate region seemed to extend farther than the eye could reach, without grandeur, without even the dignity of mountain wildness, yet striking, from the huge proportion which it seemed to bear to such more favoured spots of country as were adapted to cultivation, and fitted for the support of man; and thereby impressing irresistibly the mind of the spectator with a sense of the omnipotence of nature, and the comparative inefficacy of the boasted means of amelioration which man is capable of opposing to the disadvantages of climate and soil.[7]

It is just such passages of description which made readers of a generation ago decide that Scott was unreadable. Yet, looked at again, especially in contrast with other writers, there is something impressive about his presentation of his subject and his attitude to his reader. There is no 'cleverness' about Scott, no hint of the jaunty, the cocksure or the superior. We are invited to reconstruct a landscape in our minds. It is described in some detail, a sharp contrast being made between its appearance in winter and summer. But the description is not written for purely pictorial effect: it is a landscape which holds a message for the men who come there, and for the readers who have it described for them. The energy of its winter torrents is destructive and purposeless; there is a pitiable contrast between its winter fury and its inactivity in summer. Scott's pictures of landscape often imply a commentary on the political divisions of Scotland, which were the theme of many of his novels. Cultivation, as opposed to wildness, suggested lowland civilisation as against highland violence. And the fury of the Highlanders in war, which had something wildly impressive about it, could be contrasted with their squalid inertia in times of peace.

In this description, Scott is at pains to emphasise the comparative feebleness of human efforts at improvement in the face of a landscape which is hostile or indifferent. There is no suggestion that there is anything fictional about this landscape: his characters may be fictions but they are set in the world of real humanity, and their actions are representative of the world of humankind. Scott's narrative voice is heavy and graceless, far more concerned with accurately conveying his meaning than with any merely stylistic effect. Carefully attended to, his sprawling sentences, expressing their meaning by gradual syntactic extension until their point is laboriously made, convey the sense of a man patiently translating a landscape into an idea.

The paragraph which follows emphasises the sense of solitude which is to be found in such deserted places, whether in Scotland or Arabia, even among a company of people travelling together. The passage leads directly to a description of the feelings of the character whom Scott uses as the participating observer of the action of the novel, the young moderate Morton, who is aware of the conflicting forces in his society and who wants to avoid being destroyed by the conflict. Here is how Scott connects landscape and figure:

It was not, therefore, without a peculiar feeling of emotion, that Morton beheld, at the distance of about half a mile, the body of the cavalry to which his escort belonged, creeping up a steep and winding path which ascended from the more level moor into the hills. Their numbers, which appeared formidable when they crowded through narrow roads, and seemed multiplied by appearing partially, and at different points, among the trees, were now apparently diminished by being exposed at once to view, and in a landscape whose extent bore such immense proportion to the columns of horses and men, which, showing more like a drove of black cattle than a body of soldiers, crawled slowly along the face of the hill, their force and their numbers seeming trifling and contemptible.

'Surely', said Morton to himself, 'a handful of resolute men may defend any defile in these mountains against such a small force as this is, providing that their bravery is equal to their enthusiasm.'[8]

Scott has carefully limited his observations about the landscape to the story he is telling, since in the description of warfare landscape is part of the story. As the body of men he is describing leave the protection of the lowlands, they are dwarfed by the size and the formlessness of the landscape they are entering. Scott's comparison of them to 'a drove of black cattle' suggests their vulnerability. He has led us (and the reader of 1816 for whom he was writing) to a gradual realisation of the dangers to which British troops could be exposed in the Highlands of Scotland; he has made a native landscape seem unfamiliar and threatening by attending to its manifest and everyday features. Scott's narrative voice is serious and reflective; his attention is completely absorbed by his material; he tries to interest his reader in the exactness of his observations. Scott has plenty of liveliness and humour, but these qualities are not to be found in his narrative style. He expects from his reader disciplined and reflective attention to a philosophical attempt to discern some pattern in the events of history, which was one of his deepest concerns.

For a final, very different example of 'the narrative voice', consider this passage from *Pendennis* (1850) by W. M. Thackeray (1811–63):

Every man, however brief or inglorious may have been his academical career, must remember with kindness and tenderness the old university comrades and days. The young man's life is just beginning: the boy's leading strings are cut, and he has all the novel delights and dignities of freedom. He has no idea of cares yet, or of bad health, or of roguery, or poverty, or tomorrow's disappointment. The play has not been acted so often as to make him tired. Though the after-drink, as we mechanically go on repeating it, is stale and bitter, how pure and brilliant was that first sparkling draught of pleasure! – How the boy rushes at the cup, and with what a wild eagerness he drains it. But old epicures who are cut off from the delights of the table, and are restricted to a poached egg and a glass of water, like to see people with good appetites; and as the next best thing to being amused at a pantomime one's self is to see one's children enjoy it, I hope there may be no degree of age or experience to which mortal may attain, when he shall become such a glum philosopher, as not to be pleased with the sight of happy youth. Coming back a few weeks since from a brief visit to the old University of Oxbridge where my friend Mr. Arthur Pendennis passed some period of his life, I made the journey in the railroad by the side of a young fellow at present a student of St. Boniface. He had got an *exeat* somehow, and was bent on a day's lark in London: he never stopped rattling and talking from the commencement of the journey until its close (which was a great deal too soon for me, for I never was tired of listening to the honest young fellow's jokes and cheery laughter); and when we arrived at the terminus nothing would satisfy him but a Hansom cab, so that he might get into town the quicker, and plunge into the pleasures awaiting him there. Away the young lad went whirling, with joy lighting up his honest face; and as for the reader's humble servant, having but a small carpet bag, I got up on the outside of the omnibus, and sate there very contentedly between a Jew-pedlar smoking bad cigars, and a gentleman's servant taking care of a poodle-dog, until we got our fated complement of passengers and boxes, when the coachman drove leisurely away. *We* weren't in a hurry to get to town. Neither one of us was particularly eager about rushing into that near smoking Babylon, or thought of dining at the Club that night, or dancing at the Casino. Yet a few years more, and my young friend of the railroad will not be a whit more eager.[9]

Here is 'philosophising' of quite a different kind. Modern readers may not care for the direct appearance of the author in this way. The narrative voice of Thackeray has a meditative weariness which ruefully becomes sagging human flesh and sits on the exposed top seat of an omnibus. Thackeray presents himself, as author, as a shabby-genteel, middle-aged man, battered by life, disillusioned but not so cynical as to think that the pleasures of youth are worthless. Fashionable theories of the novel do not care for the intrusive author, but perhaps our comparisons have shown that, however objective the author tries to be, it is extraordinarily difficult to eliminate his personal style which is the medium, the substance, out of which event, character and plot are woven.

5 *The Novel and the Story*

A story has no beginning or end: arbitrarily one chooses that moment of experience from which to look back or from which to look ahead. I say 'one chooses' with the inaccurate pride of a professional writer who – when he has been seriously noted at all – has been praised for his technical ability, but do I in fact of my own will *choose* that black wet January night on the Common, in 1946, the sight of Henry Miles slanting across the wide river of rain, or did these images choose me?[1]

It is in this way that the narrator of *The End of the Affair* (1951), by Graham Greene (1904–   ), begins to tell the story he wishes to unfold. The narrator, who is telling his story in the first person, is supposed to be a novelist himself, and is therefore aware of the problems of telling a story. We are not here concerned with the interesting psychological question of where, and in what form, the novelist's material comes from. The student of the novel is more concerned with how he arranges it. At what point will the novel be deemed to begin? When will the novelist choose to linger over the scenes he is creating; when will it be sufficient to summarise the events which have brought his characters to the point from which the novel begins; will the action be reported as it is known in hindsight and in its completeness; will it be recounted step-by-step in a linear fashion, or will there be foreshadowings, or even revelations of the outcome? Any set of imagined people have relationships and experiences stretching back into the past and across an intricate web of possible associations. How is the novelist to draw a satisfactory circle round his material which will separate what is to be told from what is not?

The aim of this chapter is to look closely at two novels in order to discover how the novelist has shaped the raw material of his novel – the story or stories of which it is constructed – so that the final product has a distinctive shape and character. Let us begin with Jane Austen's *Pride and Prejudice* (1813). As the quotation above from Graham Greene may have suggested, the fundamental idea of 'story' is something which happens in a linear time-scale; 'story' in its simplest form is a series of events linked roughly by 'and then'. It would be very difficult to write a novel in this way. How would one decide what unit of behaviour was to constitute an event? To describe the events of one day might require a whole book. In his novel *Ulysses* (1918), James Joyce did try to do justice to the events of a single day in the lives of a selected group of characters, and his account of them runs to about one thousand pages. Even so, of course, his narrative is necessarily selective, especially since his idea of 'event' includes the thoughts, day-dreams, dreams and fantasies of some of his characters. A much earlier French writer, Marivaux (1688–1763), ends Book One of his novel, *The Life of Marianne* (1731), by showing Marianne preparing to go to church one morning. But the day in which she does this does not end until the last page of Book Three more than one hundred pages later. Perhaps it is not surprising that Marivaux never managed to finish his novel.

There are two problems which we have uncovered here: the first is the selection of the details of the story, the establishment of the raw material of events out of which the novel is to be made; the second is the ordering of these details. The ordering process, however, must be governed by some principle or method. The novelist must have a reason for organising the material as he (or she) does. We have chosen to use the word 'event' to suggest the primitive stuff out of which the novel has been made, but a more appropriate one is 'action' since these events are usually brought about by human agents. Sometimes a novelist allows a character to be affected in some quite arbitrary way, as if he were a falling rock or a thunder clap. A famous example is E. M. Forster's treatment of a character in *The Longest Journey* (1907), in which we are informed without any warning, 'Gerald died that afternoon. He was broken up in the football match.' Events of that kind happen in novels as in life; more common are human actions, involving promises, proposals, plans, persuasions and purposes of all kinds. It is out of these that the stories are made, and it is from stories – chains of actions linked by cause and time – that novels are formed.

Pride and Prejudice: Narrative as Discovery

Pride and Prejudice has a number of stories: principally, it concerns the experiences of the Bennet sisters and their relationships with the men they are to marry. They become involved mainly with a group of people, of more elevated social situation than themselves, who come to live on one of the estates near the village of Longbourn, where the Bennets are 'the principal inhabitants'. Another family, that of Sir William and Lady Lucas whose daughter Charlotte is a friend of Elizabeth Bennet's, is also involved in the tale. The novel begins with the arrival of Mr Bingley, 'a young man of large fortune from the North of England', at Netherfield Park which is 'let at last' and the expectation of Mrs Bennet, that one of her daughters might marry him, provides one of the main stories of the book. But the events that occur sometime in the Autumn at Meryton and continue until just before the Christmas of the following year are determined by many circumstances stretching much further back in time. It is the chance collision of these families and their histories which provides the substance of the novel. Our interest is in the way Jane Austen arranges her material into the unique and distinctive form of *Pride and Prejudice*.

A further strand of story material arises from the fact that Mr Bennet has no son to succeed him and that according to the law his estate cannot pass to his daughters. This brings Mr Collins, the nearest male heir, into the story of the Bennet family. It is a matter of chance – or rather of Jane Austen's contrivance – that Mr Collins's patron, Lady Catherine de Bourgh, is the influential aunt of Mr Bingley's best friend, Mr Darcy, who is one of the early visitors to Netherfield Park.

Mr Collins's arrival is succeeded almost immediately by the appearance of Mr Wickham, who is to be attached to the regiment quartered in the district, whose officers provide an inexhaustible source of gossip to the two youngest daughters of the family. To Elizabeth Bennet, the second of the Bennet daughters, who is the central character of the novel, Mr Wickham's interest is in his story of neglect and ill-treatment by Mr Darcy whose father had brought Wickham up and promised to provide him with a place in the Church of England. Both of these characters provide fresh material for the novel. They have their own histories; they extend the potential scope of the novel in space and time. Mr Collins's legal position affords him a strong connection with the Bennets, his link with Mr Darcy's aunt provides him with some slight connection with Mr Darcy. Lady Catherine, it appears, is concerned with Darcy not just as a nephew but as a possible husband for her own daughter. Mr Wickham's previous experiences connect him unhappily with Darcy, but his own youthful enthusiasm and good looks give him an added attraction which affects not only the rather headstrong and silly members of the Bennet family but even Elizabeth herself. The interest of the novel for the reader is just how this rich material, which offers so many possibilities for development, will be handled. According to what principle will Jane Austen shape it into a novel for our instruction and delight?

Jane Austen manages the opening section of her novel by developing three of her strands of narrative. Firstly, our attention is engaged by the relationship of the two oldest Bennet girls, Jane and Elizabeth, to the young men, Bingley and Darcy, who have come to the neighbourhood. Secondly, the arrival of Mr Collins, who has come in search of a wife, initially raises the question of which of the Bennet girls he will marry. Thirdly, the predicament of Wickham arouses the sympathies of Elizabeth Bennet, while Darcy's pride repels her and Mr Collins's proposal of marriage fills her with amused contempt. One further element of the story is the developing attachment of Jane Bennet and Mr Bingley, which gives Mrs Bennet grounds for hope that Mr Bingley might ask Jane to marry him. What we see happening in the novel is that the initial state of equilibrium of the village is upset by the arrival of a succession of young men. To put it another way, Jane Austen begins her novel by presenting her readers with a closed system — established families harmoniously under the control of their respective parents — which is ready to be broken because the daughters of the families are of marriageable age. As soon as possible marriage partners appear the underlying instability of the initial position is made clear, and we shall not be satisfied until a new equilibrium has been established, until, that is, a new set of independent families has been brought into being. The ruling principle which guides the development of Jane Austen's novel is a consideration of how such marriage relationships are satisfactorily concluded. Jane Austen ends the first volume of her novel by bringing one of the stories she has set in motion to a conclusion. Elizabeth refuses Mr Collins and he then asks Charlotte Lucas to marry him. Charlotte accepts. Of course, the marriage of Mr Bennet's heir to a woman outside the family increases the instability of the Bennet girls' position. They must marry or, on Mr Bennet's death, be beggars.

Charlotte Lucas has succeeded in securing her future by marrying, but to what kind of marriage will it lead? Jane Austen says of Charlotte:

> Without thinking highly either of men or of matrimony, marriage had always been her object; it was the only honourable provision for well-educated young women of small fortune, and however uncertain of giving happiness, must be their pleasantest preservative from want. This preservative she had now obtained; and at the age of twenty-seven, without having ever been handsome, she felt all the good luck of it.[2]

Jane Austen's treatment of Charlotte's engagement is ironic. Every sentence of this paragraph suggests the meanness of Charlotte's prize and the narrowness of her ambition. But it has its pathos, too; the situation of an unmarried woman was not to be envied. As Charlotte says of herself:

> 'I am not romantic, you know. I never was. I ask only a comfortable house; and considering Mr. Collins's character, connections, and situation in life, I am convinced that my chance of happiness with him is as fair as most people can boast on entering the marriage state.'
> Elizabeth quietly answered 'Undoubtedly.'[3]

No doubt there are many ways in which Jane Austen might have shaped her novel. What gives *Pride and Prejudice* point and direction is her concentration upon the significance of the marriage-choice. Charlotte Lucas's choice has been wholly prudential. None of her reasons for choosing Mr Collins is intrinsic to the man himself. Both she and Elizabeth know this, and the knowledge spoils their friendship:

> Between Elizabeth and Charlotte there was a restraint which kept them mutually silent on the subject; and Elizabeth felt persuaded that no real confidence could ever subsist between them again.[4]

A few pages earlier Jane Austen has recorded Elizabeth's opinion of Charlotte's choice;

> She had always felt that Charlotte's opinion of matrimony was not

exactly like her own, but she could not have supposed that when called into action, she would have sacrificed every better feeling to worldly advantage. Charlotte the wife of Mr. Collins, was a most humiliating picture! – And to the pang of a friend disgracing herself and sunk in her esteem, was added the distressing conviction that it was impossible for that friend to be tolerably happy in the lot she had chosen.[5]

Charlotte's action in choosing Mr Collins takes the reader back to a conversation between her and Elizabeth recorded in Chapter Six, when they are discussing the possibility of a match between Jane and Bingley. There Charlotte says:

'I wish Jane success with all my heart; and if she were married to him tomorrow, I should think she had as good a chance of happiness, as if she were to be studying his character for a twelve-month. Happiness in marriage is entirely a matter of chance. If the dispositions of the parties are ever so well known to each other, or ever so similar beforehand, it does not advance their felicity in the least. They always continue to grow sufficiently unlike afterwards to have their share of vexation; and it is better to know as little as possible of the defects of the person with whom you are to pass your life.'
'You make me laugh, Charlotte; [Elizabeth replies] but it is not sound. You know it is not sound, and that you would never act in this way yourself.'[6]

The real cynicism of Charlotte's attitude is reflected in her remark (earlier in Chapter Six), 'If a woman conceals her affection from the object of it, she may lose the opportunity of fixing him . . . . In nine cases out of ten, a woman had better show *more* affection than she feels.' It may well be that this is an attitude born of despair of meeting a man who suits her, but for Charlotte the only success is the capture of a husband. Elizabeth has other views: for her, nothing is worth the sacrifice of the integrity of her own feelings, her own sense of the genuineness of the attachment that people feel for one another. The word 'attachment' carries a special weight of meaning: it signifies a conscious mutual sharing of interests and values. It does not suggest anything calculating, or coldly intellectual. There is spontaneity, a sense of mutual recognition and trust, and an implicit commitment to life-long companionship.

This high ideal of a possible human relationship is indeed the subject matter of *Pride and Prejudice*: pride and prejudice are only two of the attitudes which might prevent young people attaining it. The same question is posed of all the central characters in the novel: to what extent have they discovered this key to a successful life? Now we have moved away from the surface level of event and episode. We are looking at deeper layers of meaning and intention as they are revealed in the novel. As we look more carefully at the action of the novel we begin to see how the behaviour of the characters, their choices and decisions, and the depth in which they are considered are controlled by principles of composition which serve the themes the novelist wishes to explore.

Let us consider in just a little more detail the first volume of *Pride and Prejudice*, which consists of the first twenty-three chapters of the novel. The first four chapters describe the arrival of Bingley and his party to Netherfield and the initial impressions which the Bennets have of them. In Chapter Five Sir William Lucas and his family are introduced; in Chapter Seven we hear more of Catherine and Lydia Bennet and their interest in the officers quartered in the local town, but most of that chapter and the five that follow are concerned with Jane's unfortunate visit to Netherfield and her detention there with the cold she caught after she was drenched on her way. In Chapter Thirteen Mr Collins makes his arrival; in Chapter Fifteen Mr Wickham joins the officers at Meryton. In Chapter Sixteen the question of Wickham's previous relationship with Darcy is raised and continued in Chapter Eighteen. Chapter Nineteen begins the story of Mr Collins's attempt to find a wife among the Bennet girls and ends with his settling for Charlotte Lucas. By the end of the volume we have seen the introduction of all the principal characters and the main material out of which the novel is to be fashioned. Much of this 'story-stuff' is generated by Wickham. Those chapters in which the question of his relationship with Darcy is first raised generate misunderstandings between Elizabeth and Darcy, which are not finally cleared up until the twelfth chapter of Volume Two (Chapter Thirty-five), when Elizabeth is forced to revise her view of the relative worth of Wickham and Darcy. The final development of this material occurs in the third volume of the novel, when in the fourth chapter (Chapter Forty-six) a letter from Jane brings news of Wickham's elopement with Lydia.

But what principles determine the selection and arrangement of the material of the novel? If the desired aim of the characters is to find a life partner who will conform to certain ideal standards of behaviour, part of the novelist's task is to show us the features of the type of character she has in mind. Jane Austen works mainly by contrast. Wickham and Darcy are set against one another as examples of honesty and dishonesty, of candour and deceit, of reliability and untrustworthiness. Jane Austen intensifies the contrast between them by bringing them into direct relationship with one another: Wickham shows his baseness and ingratitude by his unsuccessful attempt to seduce Darcy's sister; Darcy shows his magnanimity by helping to arrange Lydia's marriage after Wickham has eloped with her.

The valuation and re-valuation of the characters of Wickham and Darcy is a process that takes place in Elizabeth Bennet's mind. She is the character who is most fully revealed to us in this novel. The reader is allowed to share her hopes, her fears and, above all, her misjudgements. Jane Austen's novel proceeds by a method of classification: along with Elizabeth, the reader gradually becomes clearer about matters of factual truth and about matters of moral truth. As we become clearer about what Wickham and Darcy have actually done, so we become clearer about the kind of men they are and about the moral standards by which they live. Part of her way of telling a story depends on the unveiling of what has remained hidden. To some extent it resembles the method of the writer of detective stories. In many of her novels there is an element of mystery: secrets of character or of relationships are revealed in the course of the novel. Jane Austen sows these seeds of mystery and allows them to develop into mature growths, as she does with Wickham's story that Darcy cheated him out of a legacy. But she does not do this simply to mystify the reader, as a writer of detective fiction might do. Her purpose is to exercise the powers of judgement of her own characters, and in doing so, to suggest more and less successful ways of forming judgements. Forming good relationships is the main life-task she sets her characters: forming good judgements about people is a vitally necessary instrument for performing it.

In the second volume of *Pride and Prejudice* Elizabeth is forced to think most carefully about the relative merits of Wickham and Darcy. In the eleventh chapter of the volume (Chapter Thirty-four) she refuses Darcy's unexpected proposal of marriage with an uncompromising hostility, which is partly based on the accusations Wickham has made against him. Darcy's reply to these accusations makes painful reading, and Elizabeth recollects that she knows virtually nothing about Wickham:

Of his former way of life, nothing had been known in Hertfordshire but what he told himself. As to his real character, had information been in her power, she had never felt a wish of enquiring. His countenance, voice and manner, had established him at once in the possession of every virtue. She tried to recollect some instance of goodness, some distinguished trait of integrity or benevolence, that might rescue him from the attacks of Mr. Darcy; or, at least, by the predominance of virtue, atone for those casual errors under which she would endeavour to class, what Mr. Darcy had described as the idleness and vice of many years continuance. But no such recollection befriended her. She could see him instantly before her, in every charm of air and address; but she could remember no more substantial good than the general approbation of the neighbourhood, and the regard which his social powers had gained him in the mess.[7]

Jane Austen evokes excellently the strange process of evaluating another person, of estimating the likely character of an acquaintance. (How well she suggests the almost hallucinatory way in which Elizabeth Bennet summons Wickham before her so that she can inspect him with her mind's eye.) In the process of judging Wickham, Elizabeth finds out something about herself: her approval of him was based on very little but the impression she had formed of his good looks and agreeable manners. This is how Jane Austen describes her moment of self-discovery:

She grew absolutely ashamed of herself. – Of neither Darcy nor Wickham could she think, without feeling that she had been blind, partial, prejudiced, absurd.

'How despicably have I acted!' she cried. – 'I, who have prided myself on my discernment! – I, who have valued myself on my abilities! who have often disdained the generous candour of my sister, and gratified my vanity, in useless or blameable distrust. – How humiliating is this discovery! – Yes, how just a humiliation! – Had I been in love, I could not have been more wretchedly blind. But vanity, not love, has been my folly. – Pleased with the preference of one, and offended by the neglect of the other, on the very beginning of our acquaintance, I have courted prepossession and ignorance, and driven reason away, where either were concerned. Till this moment, I never knew myself.'[8]

The contrast between Wickham and Darcy is continued in this passage of reflection. On first acquaintance Wickham liked her and showed his liking, Darcy did not. Elizabeth now reproaches herself for returning these feelings unthinkingly and for failing to notice that liking and approval need not be the same.

Having reorganised her opinion about Darcy's character, can she re-establish her relationship with him? That question dominates the third volume of the novel, though Elizabeth Bennet does not quite put it that way herself. When a change of plans brings her to Darcy's house, her only concern is that she should not meet him. When she does, she is afraid he will think that she is throwing herself in his way. The final reconciliation of Elizabeth and Darcy is postponed by the elopement of Wickham and Lydia, and by the intervention of Darcy's aunt, Lady Catherine de Bourgh, who wants Darcy for her own daughter. The encounter between Elizabeth and Lady Catherine is a celebrated scene, which well displays the outrageous egotism of the latter and the firm self-confidence of the former. But the scene between these two high-sprited ladies is not simply one of the comic highlights of the novel; it also helps to motivate Darcy. It is when he hears that Elizabeth has refused to promise not to enter into an engagement with him that he is encouraged to propose to her for a second time.

Elizabeth's own expectation of what might happen is very different: she believes that Lady Catherine will persuade her nephew not to have anything more to do with her:

> She knew not the exact degree of his affection for his aunt, or his dependence on her judgement, but it was natural to suppose that he thought much higher of her ladyship than *she* could do; and it was certain, that in enumerating the miseries of a marriage with *one*, whose immediate connections were so unequal to his own, his aunt would address him on his weakest side. With all his notions of dignity . . . . If he had been wavering before, as to what he should do, which had often seemed likely, the advice and intreaty of so near a relation might settle every doubt, and determine him at once to be as happy, as dignity unblemished could make him. In that case he would return no more.[9]

But Elizabeth's expectations turn out to be wrong: Darcy's opinion of his aunt is very different from what she believes it to be. Elizabeth's reflections on Darcy remind us of the limitations of our knowledge of others. Much of our expectations about how others will behave are based on oversimplified stereotypes. Reason how we may, our knowledge, even if not vitiated by pride and prejudice, is incomplete. Our knowledge of others must be built on what they do in specific situations; it is in close contact with their particular words and actions that we come to understand them. But acquaintance by itself perhaps is not enough. There must be some measure of sympathy and understanding. Caroline Bingley has many opportunities to get to know Mr Darcy, but she fails to understand him.

If we ask what it is in Elizabeth Bennet that Darcy finds so attractive, we are compelled to return to those chapters in the novel which describe Elizabeth's visit to Netherfield, when Jane is laid up in bed with her cold. Once again, Jane Austen contrasts one character with another to establish the kind of person whom we ought to admire. Elizabeth's temporary residence at Netherfield Park allows the reader (and Mr Darcy) many opportunities of comparing her with the ladies of Netherfield, in particular with Caroline. Consider a fairly lengthy section from Chapter Eleven. Miss Bingley has persuaded Elizabeth to walk about the room with her. Darcy, who is present, is perfectly well aware that she wants to attract his attention, and he tells her so:

'Oh! shocking!' cried Miss Bingley. 'I have never heard anything so abominable. How shall we punish him for such a speech?'

'Nothing so easy, if you have but the inclination,' said Elizabeth. 'We can all plague and punish one another. Teaze him — laugh at him. — Intimate as you are, you must know how it is to be done.'

'But upon my honour I do *not*. I do assure you that my intimacy has not yet taught me *that*. Teaze calmness of temper and presence of mind! No, no — I feel he may defy us there. And as to laughter, we will not expose ourselves, if you please, by attempting to laugh without a subject. Mr. Darcy may hug himself.'

'Mr. Darcy is not to be laughed at!' cried Elizabeth. 'That is an uncommon advantage, and uncommon I hope it will continue, for it would be a great loss to *me* to have many such acquaintance. I dearly love a laugh.'

'Miss Bingley,' he said, 'has given me credit for more than can be. The wisest and best of men, nay the wisest and best of their actions, may be rendered ridiculous by a person whose first object in life is a joke.'

'Certainly,' replied Elizabeth — 'there are such people, but I hope

I am not one of *them*. I hope I never ridicule what is wise or good. Follies and nonsense, whims and inconsistencies do divert me, I own, and I laugh at them whenever I can. – But these, I suppose, are precisely what you are without.'[10]

'Perhaps that is not possible for anyone. But it has been often the study of my life to avoid those weaknesses which often expose a strong understanding to ridicule.'

'Such as vanity and pride.'

'Yes, vanity is a weakness indeed. But pride – where there is a real superiority of mind – pride will always be under good regulation.'

Elizabeth turned away to hide a smile.

'Your examination of Mr. Darcy is over, I presume,' said Miss Bingley; – 'and pray what is the result?'

'I am perfectly convinced by it that Mr. Darcy has no defect. He owns it himself without disguise.'[11]

A conversation of this sort displays literary skill of the highest order; it not only clarifies relationships, it advances them. Notice, first of all, Miss Bingley's use of language: when she talks of 'punishing' Darcy, she has no clear intention behind the word. She is shocked when Elizabeth makes it clear that such a word might have a definite meaning and the action it refers to a definite place in human behaviour. Miss Bingley uses language to disguise her intentions (though she is rarely successful in doing so); Elizabeth uses language to analyse the reality of how people behave to one another. Notice too how Miss Bingley implicitly admits that she does not know Darcy well enough to laugh at him. She suggests she would not dare take such a liberty. His 'calmness of temper and presence of mind' would be too strong a defence for her to penetrate. Darcy is much too clever to allow her to get near to him. The reader will have noticed this already in a direct and almost embarrassing way. Remember the telling incident at the entertainment given by Sir William Lucas, when Darcy dares to tell Miss Bingley of his admiration for Elizabeth. The conversation is in Chapter Six, where Miss Bingley says:

'I can guess the subject of your reverie.'

'I should imagine not.'

'You are considering how insupportable it would be to pass many evenings in this manner – in such society; and indeed I am quite of your opinion. I was never more annoyed! The insipidity and yet the noise; the nothingness and yet the self-importance of all these people! – What would I give to hear your strictures on them!'

'Your conjecture is totally wrong, I assure you. My mind was more agreeably engaged. I have been meditating on the very great pleasure which a pair of fine eyes in the face of a pretty woman can bestow.'

Miss Bingley immediately fixed her eyes on his face, and desired he would tell her what lady had the credit of inspiring such reflections. Mr. Darcy replied with great intrepidity:

'Miss Elizabeth Bennet.'

'Miss Elizabeth Bennet!' repeated Miss Bingley. 'I am all astonishment. How long has she been a favourite? – and pray when am I to wish you joy?'[12]

If the reader sometimes thinks that Jane Austen writes dialogue as if for a chess-match, Miss Bingley here utters her last remark with the foolhardiness of a player who makes a threatening move just after he has lost his queen. The way Jane Austen – poor, plain, old-maidish Jane, as some readers may think her – makes Miss Bingley switch off speech and switch on her own no doubt magnificent eyes at Darcy is a remarkable stroke of art – all the more remarkable for not being subtle. We must share Miss Bingley's inward pang as her vulnerability to the not-quite-delivered compliment is revealed, only to be succeeded by the exposure of her vulnerability to an insult which Darcy scarcely troubles to withhold. Jane Austen praises Darcy's boldness in daring to compliment Elizabeth instead of offering Caroline Bingley the compliment she expects for herself – but it is a courage that takes little account of Miss Bingley's feelings.

When we return to Elizabeth Bennet's conversation with Darcy, we find that in contrast she is well able to cope with him. Their rapid exchange appears superficial enough at first. But it goes to the heart of each character's most firmly held values. Elizabeth's laughter is not heartless; it is directed against 'follies and nonsense, whims and inconsistencies'. In trying to avoid her challenge that he suffers from vanity or pride (or both), Darcy falls into just the kind of inconsistency that makes Elizabeth Bennet laugh. In asserting that 'a real superiority of mind' will always keep pride in check, he appears vain enough to believe that he *is* so superior.

But this cut and thrust of conversation is lost on Caroline Bingley.

When Darcy protests that he did not mean to argue that he was perfect, he puts it this way:

'I have faults enough, but they are not, I hope, of understanding. My temper I dare not vouch for. – It is I believe too little yielding – certainly too little for the convenience of the world. I cannot forget the follies and vices of others soon as I ought, nor their offences against myself. My feelings are not puffed about with every attempt to move them. My temper would perhaps be called resentful. – My good opinion once lost is lost forever.'

'That is a failing indeed!' – cried Elizabeth. 'Implacable resentment *is* a shade in character. But you have chosen your fault well. – I really cannot *laugh* at it. You are safe from me.'

'There is, I believe, in every disposition a tendency to some particular evil, a natural defect, which not even the best education can overcome.'

'And *your* defect is a propensity to hate everybody.'

'And yours,' he replied with a smile, 'is wilfully to misunderstand them.'

'Do let us have a little music,' cried Miss Bingley, tired of a conversation in which she had no share.[13]

Poor Caroline is left out because she has not the intelligence to join in. We must not forget that, although Darcy began by believing that Elizabeth's face was quite unremarkable in appearance, 'he began to find it was rendered uncommonly intelligent by the beautiful expression of her dark eyes'. Beauty and intelligence, here, are hardly to be distinguished from one another. Elizabeth's conversations with Darcy – and this is an excellent example – are extremely rapid, penetrating and intelligent. Darcy's self-justification is a kind of self-exposure. The unbending consistency he prides himself on is too serious a failing to be laughed at. 'Implacable resentment' has a touch of the satanic about it; its quality of feeling is too extreme for the reasonable good sense we expect of the hero of a novel by Jane Austen. Darcy wishes to excuse his fault of character by seeing it as something innate which cannot be altered; he suggests that it is the specific character found in him of the original sin common to all human beings. Elizabeth suggests that on the contrary any defect can be corrected, if it is clearly recognised for what it is.

By the end of this conversation a very considerable intimacy has been achieved. Their conversation has been conducted in a serious way which goes beyond mere social exchange. Just as their sentences mesh closely together, so their spirits begin to link closely too. When Caroline Bingley calls for music, we may imagine that she can just sense how difficult it will be to sever the bond that is beginning to form between Elizabeth and Darcy.

The knowledge which one person gains of another can only be formed over a period of time; it is fragmentary, partial and conjectural. Direct experience of the other may have to be compared with the opinions formed by other people, whose judgements may be more or less trustworthy. Knowledge of the present has also to be compared with knowledge of the past, which is likely to be even more indirect and uncertain. The principle which directs the events of *Pride and Prejudice* is the author's interest in discovering how hero and heroine come to know one another. If Elizabeth believes Wickham's account of his early relationship with Darcy, she may be willing to believe that Darcy's 'implacable resentment' may be aroused unjustly, that he has in his disposition 'a propensity to hate everybody'. (Her judgement is an excellent example of how easily we may transform a particular instance into a general rule.) But is Wickham a reliable witness? Elizabeth's experience of him has been most pleasant; she has very favourable impressions of him. But these impressions are misleading: Elizabeth has to learn that true knowledge is based not on impression but on a much more complex understanding of people and their circumstances, which can only be attained by thoughtful and critical attention.

Elizabeth learns to understand Darcy in two ways: first, by the kind of personal involvement which we have been studying, an involvement particularly in argument which allows them to probe and sift each other's language, as the best way of attaining some knowledge of the character and complexion of one another's mind. And, second, by setting this personal knowledge in the context of a less direct knowledge of the experiences which have formed his character and dispositions – in other words, by coming to understand something of Darcy's history. Two long letters in the novel – the first from Darcy himself, which he gives to Elizabeth just after she has rejected his proposal of marriage (Chapter Thirty-five), the second from her aunt, Mrs Gardiner, which tells her how Darcy behaved towards Wickham and Lydia in London (Chapter Fifty-two) – reveal to Elizabeth and to the reader aspects of Darcy's life and character which no direct present experience of him could have done. The same of course is true of the description of Darcy as a boy supplied by the housekeeper at Pemberley (Chapter Forty-three).

In the way she tells her story, then, Jane Austen contrasts two ways of knowing – the direct, emotionally charged knowledge produced by immediate experience and the indirect, more analytical knowledge produced by reasoned reflection. The immediacy of direct experience is contrasted with the gradual unfolding of the knowledge of the past. In telling the story as she does, Jane Austen prompts us to reflect upon themes which go beyond the events she is narrating; we are led to consider the need for continuity and cohesiveness in the conduct of life and the danger of being too much at the mercy of immediate events. This theme emerges strikingly in the second serious conversation which Elizabeth and Darcy have. It takes place at the Netherfield ball described in Chapter Eighteen. They have proceeded from silence to stilted conversation about conventional themes and then to the more serious – though never humourless – teasing, by which Elizabeth probes Darcy's real character. Then Elizabeth says:

'We have tried two or three subjects already without success, and what are we to talk of next. I cannot imagine.'

'What think you of books?' said he, smiling.

'Books – Oh! no – I am sure we never read the same, or not with the same feelings.'

'I am sorry you think so; but if that be the case, there can be no want of subject. – We may compare our different opinions.'

'No – I cannot talk of books in a ball-room; my head is always full of something else.'

'The *present* always occupies you in such scenes – does it?' said he, with a look of doubt.

'Yes, always,' she replied, without knowing what she said, for her thoughts had wandered far from the subject, as soon afterwards appeared by her suddenly exclaiming, 'I remember hearing you once say, Mr. Darcy, that you hardly ever forgave, that your resentment once created was unappeasable. You are very cautious, I suppose, as to its *being created*.'

'I am,' said he, with a firm voice.

'And never allow yourself to be blinded by prejudice?'

'I hope not.'

'It is particularly incumbent on those who never change their opinion, to be secure of judging properly at first.'

'May I ask to what these questions tend?'

'Merely to the illustration of *your* character,' said she, endeavouring to shake off her gravity. 'I am trying to make it out.'

'And what is your success?'

She shook her head. 'I do not get on at all. I hear such different accounts of you as puzzle me exceedingly.'[14]

Such a passage is worth careful attention. Elizabeth's teasing is sometimes an instrument of her serious purposes. She pretends to be giving Darcy a verbal sketch of his character, but it concerns her that the portrait should be accurate. Unlike physical features, character, motive and disposition are not aspects of the person which are open to immediate view. Jane Austen ensures that the reader does not misjudge Elizabeth: although she says she is preoccupied with the present, she clearly shows she has been thinking of the past, and indeed of her past experience of Darcy. She is not tied to immediate sensation: she is actively concerned to link the present and the past, to construct out of her own impressions, as well as from the reports she has received from others, a coherent picture of Darcy. The registering, the ordering and re-ordering of information about others are recurrent actions in this novel which give it a distinctive pattern and rhythm.

What we have found in considering *Pride and Prejudice* is that a novel is very far from being a story: we can make a distinction between the events and circumstances which provide the novelist with his or her material and the ways in which the material is treated. The method of publication of *Pride and Prejudice* in three volumes has influenced the way the novelist has shaped it in three consecutive and cumulative sections. The first of these ends with Elizabeth's refusal to marry Mr Collins, the acceptance of him by Charlotte Lucas and the uncertainty about Bingley's interest in Jane. The second volume of the novel consists of journeys: Jane visits London; Elizabeth visits the new Mrs Collins. It reaches a climax in Elizabeth's refusal of Mr Darcy and ends with her preparing to visit Derbyshire with her aunt and uncle. The final volume is one of interruptions, of surprise, confusion and suspense. Elizabeth's visit to Pemberley, which brings her again into the company of Darcy, is interrupted by news of Lydia's elopement with Wickham. Darcy's help in resolving this affair leads Elizabeth to reappraise his conduct, and, despite an unhelpful intervention by Lady Catherine de Bourgh, they are reconciled and engaged. The novel ends happily with Jane's engagement to Bingley.

Jane Austen knits the pattern of the action of the novel more firmly together by establishing links between the characters: Mr Collins has an unattractive legal link with the Bennets; through his patron, Lady Catherine, he is linked with Mr Darcy. Darcy is linked to Wickham through boyhood friendship. Elizabeth's aunt Gardiner's happy memories of Pemberley suggest Derbyshire as a suitable place for her to bring her husband and her niece on holiday. The novel begins by disrupting a settled pattern of family life and ends after establishing a quite new pattern of settled families. It introduces us to a group of girls related by family connection and girlhood friendship; during the action of the novel they are sorted out according to Jane Austen's criteria of moral worth. What she favours is a complex mixture of intelligent self-awareness, good-humour, wit and the capacity for making links with others of a similar nature. According to these criteria, Elizabeth ranks high; Mary, who displays learning without intelligence or wit, rather low. A little cruelly, perhaps, each girl is allowed to marry according to her kind (Mary, we may suspect, is unmarriageable), though the match of Jane and Bingley indicates that Jane Austen allows an honourable place to the good-looking and good-natured who marry for a love which they cannot quite put into words.

Bearing in mind the distinctions we have made between novel and story, between material and treatment, let us look now, by contrast, at quite a different novel – F. Scott Fitzgerald's *The Great Gatsby*. If the finishing point towards which *Pride and Prejudice* moves is marriage, *The Great Gatsby* moves through conflict and confusion towards death. Like *Pride and Prejudice* the action of *The Great Gatsby* carries with it a clarification; at the end of the novel the reader understands by what principles and according to what criteria its confused events and action are to be understood.

The Great Gatsby: Discovery and the Patterns of Symbolism

The Great Gatsby is a fairly short novel, consisting of nine chapters. Its action takes place in a period of time stretching from June to October 1922, but the material with which it deals stretches farther back into the past. It is set in a time of American history, just after the First World War, when the sale or manufacture of intoxicating liquors was forbidden. 'Bootlegging', or the traffic in illegal whisky was one way of making money. Unlike *Pride and Prejudice*, the action is narrated by a character who has some part to play in the novel, although his main function is as an observer and commentator. He has two styles of narration: in one, he describes in detail what happened; in the other, he summarises, fills in background detail, muses and moralises. Nick Carraway, the narrator, is a privileged young man from a wealthy background, but in the first page of the novel it is suggested that his main privilege is to have 'a sense of the fundamental decencies'. Elsewhere he congratulates himself upon his honesty.

The presence of a narrator within the novel makes some difference to its presentation and to the reader's response to it. The reader is more aware of the colour which may be added to the story by the personality of the story-teller; there may even be some question of how far we are to accept his version of events. The impersonal narration of *Pride and Prejudice* has a tone and character of its own (think, for instance, of its famous opening sentence) but its narrative voice is much less obtrusive, and it would not occur to us to challenge its judgements. Part of the effect which Fitzgerald gains from using Carraway as narrator is that he is young, inexperienced and idealistic. His narration of the events involving Jay Gatsby, Tom and Daisy Buchanan and the Wilsons tells us something about his own development. Like Elizabeth Bennet, Nick Carraway grows in awareness and in moral understanding during the course of the novel. But his understanding is gained mainly through his observation of and reflection upon the behaviour of others, whereas Elizabeth's develops through the choices and decisions she makes as a participant in the action of *Pride and Prejudice*. One difference between the two novels is that Jane Austen's narration offers a secure framework of values against which the behaviour of the characters in the novel may be judged: Nick Carraway's system of values is more personal and more tentative. But behind the narrator stands the author who has designed and written the novel: if we look carefully we may see some evidence of his values, attitudes and opinions, which, if they are not explicitly stated, as Jane Austen's are, can be detected nevertheless.

One example of this consists in Fitzgerald's using the facts of American geography (and the history of its cultural development) as a kind of positive and negative pole for the system of moral values Nick Carraway discovers for himself — as a rough-and-ready starting point let us say West means good, East means bad. Having observed the slice of New York life which the novel reveals to us, Nick Carraway concludes that it is possible to distinguish good from evil, and that it is preferable to be good. Although the action of the novel leads towards the death of the character from whom the novel takes its name, there is a positive goal for the book. The moral perceptions of Nick Carraway move from a position of neutrality to one of commitment.

East, then, in the moral geography of the novel represents confused moral values, West represents something traditional and absolute, though Fitzgerald does not spell out what his absolute system of values is. In moving from the Mid-West of America to New York to follow a career in the money markets, Nick Carraway is entering dangerous ground. Fitzgerald maintains the geographical distinction referred to already by dividing the tip of Long Island, where the action of the novel mainly takes place, into East Egg, where the Buchanans live, and West Egg, where Nick and Jay Gatsby live as neighbours. The main difficulty for the reader is to decide where Gatsby stands on the moral axis of the novel. Fitzgerald places him alongside Nick Carraway, but what exactly is his moral status? Has he the right to live in the West, and is it significant that all his thoughts and longings should be towards the East? That we can ask such questions at all points to an interesting difference between Fitzgerald's and Jane Austen's ways of organising their novels. Fitzgerald uses a method which may appear to reduce the significance which Jane Austen gave to words and deeds. Perhaps we can say that Fitzgerald is using the method of the allegorist: for him West and East have the kind of absolute value which John Bunyan gave to the Celestial City and to Vanity Fair. But there is a difference: Bunyan (and Bunyan's traditional sources) made it clear what kind of behaviour led to one place or to the other. Fitzgerald's geographical terms appear to embody absolute values, but the content of the values, what kind of behaviour would count as good rather than bad, seems less clear.

There are three interlocking strands in the narrative of *The Great Gatsby*: the principal one is Jay Gatsby's attempt to recapture Daisy Buchanan whom he had known five years before the action of the novel begins, when he was a young officer in the United States army and she was a young unmarried woman, the daughter of a rich family; the second is her husband Tom Buchanan's extra-marital affair with the wife of a garage proprietor, who lives in an unattractive suburb of New York; the third, and the least significant of the three, is Nick Carraway's attachment to Jordan Baker, one of Daisy's friends, who is a sportswoman of some reputation. Reduced to summary, the action of the novel may seem rather melodramatic. Nick Carraway is drawn into the Buchanans' circle because he is Daisy's cousin; the Buchanans' marriage has been unhappy from the start because of Tom's interest in other women; Nick is invited to join the parties thrown by Jay Gatsby, his extravagantly rich neighbour, because Gatsby wants to find a way of meeting Daisy Buchanan. After a number of meetings, which Nick arranges, Nick and Jordan, Tom and Daisy and Gatsby leave for New York. In a hotel room there Gatsby and Tom argue with one another for Daisy's affections. Tom wins, and feels strong enough to ask Gatsby to take Daisy home in his own car.

It is vital for the management of the story of this novel that on the way to New York Tom Buchanan has been driving Gatsby's car, and that Gatsby has driven Daisy in Tom Buchanan's car. On the way to New York Buchanan stopped for petrol at the garage run by Wilson, who has begun to suspect that his wife is being unfaithful with someone. The reader knows from earlier chapters that Tom Buchanan is her lover. When Mrs Wilson sees the car on its return journey, she runs out towards it, fleeing from her jealous husband. It hits her and fails to stop. Fitzgerald allows the reader to infer that Daisy has been driving the car. Next day, Wilson goes out to find the car that has killed his wife; he finds out that it was Gatsby's; he goes to West Egg and shoots him in his swimming pool.

Very little of this complex and rather implausible story of the events leading to Mrs Wilson's death and the consequent death of Gatsby is told directly in the novel. The reader has to reconstruct a coherent account of them from hints and allusions. Nick was not present when Mrs Wilson was struck by the car, so the narrative at that point is Nick's account of what was said at the inquest with some details from reports in the newspapers. Wilson had asserted his authority over his wife, and had locked her in her room; but she had escaped, and was running towards a car she thought she knew, to obtain some help. A moment later Tom Buchanan and Nick and Jordan arrive at the scene of the accident, and Nick resumes his narration. When they return home, Nick declines Tom's invitation to go into East Egg; at West Egg he finds Gatsby still anxious about Daisy. But when Nick goes over to East Egg to see what is happening there, a look through a window shows him Tom and Daisy sitting over a late supper in attitudes that suggest a complete unity of purpose. As Nick puts it, 'anybody would have said they were conspiring together'.

The story recounted here occupies Chapters Seven and Eight of

The Great Gatsby. But the complicated sequence of events is drastically simplified in the novel. With an effort of reconstruction, the reader can find out what happened, but Fitzgerald is mainly concerned to emphasise the fact that in the battle for Daisy, Tom wins because Daisy deserts Gatsby, and the Buchanans do nothing to prevent Wilson shooting Gatsby in the belief that he killed his wife. What is crucial here is not the sequence of events that leads to Gatsby's death, but the fact that he has been betrayed. The final chapter of the novel, which describes Gatsby's funeral, suggests just how complete his betrayal has been since none of the people who came to his parties comes to see him buried.

The problem of understanding *The Great Gatsby* does not lie in understanding the events of the novel: it lies in understanding their significance. In *Pride and Prejudice* the events of the novel were human actions which were to be judged according to criteria which Jane Austen makes explicit in the course of her novel. In *The Great Gatsby* some of the events – the deaths of Mrs Wilson and of Gatsby himself – have no moral significance. The central actions in the novel are Gatsby's quest for Daisy, Daisy's rejection of him and Nick's rejection of New York and what it stands for. Unlike Jane Austen, Fitzgerald does not explicitly guide the reader about how to understand his novel. He shows Nick Carraway making his own evaluation of Gatsby and his world, but he does not offer any explicit justification for Nick's view. In Chapter Eight we are told that Nick shouts at Gatsby, 'They're a rotten crowd, ... You're worth the whole damn bunch put together.' But we are not told why Nick thinks this, nor are we quite told who he means by 'the rotten crowd'. Does he mean Tom and Daisy Buchanan and their set, or the people who came to Gatsby's parties, or to Gatsby's own apparently shady associates, or all of these? There is a vagueness about Nick's judgement which the reader feels compelled to make more exact. Why does Nick reject New York, and why did Daisy reject Gatsby?

The second question must be tackled first. Nick's attitude to the moral values of the East is influenced in particular by the example of Daisy Buchanan. Daisy is the spoiled daughter of wealthy America; she is beautiful, desirable and socially successful. But it is difficult to believe that she has integrity or strength of character or any capacity for love. It might seem that Fitzgerald's shifting, pleasure-seeking world has no place for such absolutes, and yet, as Nick Carraway points out in the opening pages of the novel, tolerance has its limits.

Conduct [he says] may be founded on the hard rock or the wet marshes, but after a certain point I don't care what it's founded on. When I came back from the East last autumn [after the events recorded in the novel have taken place] I felt that I wanted the world to be in uniform and at a sort of moral attention forever; I wanted no more riotous excursions with privileged glimpses into human heart.[15]

When Nick says that he does not care what conduct is founded on, he means that there is a point where one is no longer able to afford the luxury of speculating on why people behave as they do; all that matters is that what they do is right. The metaphor of the rock which Nick uses appears several times in the novel. Here it refers to firmly based moral standards. There may be an echo of the New Testament parable about the house which is built upon rock and which survives a storm of wind and rain, while the house built on sand perishes. A second reference to a rock occurs in Chapter Two when a photograph on the wall of the sleazy flat which Tom Buchanan has rented for his mistress, Myrtle Wilson, is described as looking like 'a hen sitting on a blurred rock'. It is, however, a photograph of a stout old lady, Mrs Wilson's mother, which presides over the drunken party which ensues, like a faded relic from another era. While he is in the flat, Nick picks up a book oddly entitled *Simon Called Peter*. No explanation is given of the contents of this book, or why it should be mentioned at all; all we are told of the chapter which Nick reads is 'either it was terrible stuff or the whisky distorted things, because it didn't make sense to me'. It is difficult not to connect *Simon Called Peter* with St Peter, the Apostle, whose name in Greek meant 'rock', and on which Christ made the punning remark, 'Upon this rock I shall build my church'. In the atmosphere of Myrtle Wilson's party a book referring to these matters might make little sense, lying as it did alongside *Town Tattle* and 'some of the small scandal magazines of Broadway'.

There is one final example of the recurrent use of this word, or image, or motif. It occurs in Chapter Six in a passage which describes the very young Jay Gatsby on the verge of manhood:

But his heart was in a constant, turbulent riot. The most grotesque and fantastic conceits haunted him in his bed at night. A universe of ineffable gaudiness spun itself out in his brain while the clock ticked on the washstand and the moon soaked with wet light his tangled clothes upon the floor. Each night he added to the pattern of his fancies until drowsiness closed down upon some vivid scene with an oblivious embrace. For a while these reveries provided an outlet for his imagination; they were a satisfactory hint of the unreality of reality, a promise that the rock of the world was founded securely on a fairy's wing.[16]

Here the word 'rock' is still used to evoke ideas of stability and permanence, but Fitzgerald suggests that the source of stability lies in Gatsby's imagination, which is able to supply 'the conceits', 'the universe of ineffable gaudiness', and 'the fancies' which preoccupy him. The key to Gatsby's character is his capacity for making his dreams come true. His first conception of 'reality' had been 'the hot struggle of the poor', the class into which he was born and from which he tried to escape. Jimmy Gatz, as we learn from his father, who only arrives on the scene after Gatsby's death, transformed himself into Jay Gatsby by imagining a better way of life for himself and by creating what he had imagined. This is how Fitzgerald puts it:

The truth was that Jay Gatsby of West Egg, Long Island, sprang from his Platonic conception of himself. He was a son of God – a phrase which, if it means anything, means just that – and he must be about his Father's business, the service of a vast, vulgar, and meretricious beauty. So he invented just the sort of Jay Gatsby that a seventeen-year-old boy would be likely to invent, and to this conception he was faithful to the end.[17]

Gatsby's fidelity to his ideal gives him value in Nick's eyes: it is a kind of integrity. Daisy represents for Gatsby the fairyland world he believes to be superior to reality. But Daisy herself lives in a world where compromise has to be made. She fell in love with Gatsby as a young officer, but she failed to say goodbye to him when he went overseas, and married Tom Buchanan instead. Five years later she has the chance to declare her love for Gatsby, but again she wavers. Tom's innuendoes about the sources of Gatsby's wealth are too much for her, and she cannot honestly say she has not loved Tom too. The reader might feel a little sympathy for Daisy: Gatsby idealises her; he does not expect her to live in the world of desire, of conflicting impulse, of moral choice. She chooses Tom because he is safe and established; she is not aware of Gatsby's Platonic conception of himself, she sees only an adventurer, 'a penniless young man without a past', who has become rich by uncertain means. Timidity makes her draw back. Perhaps we can draw some rough parallel between her and Charlotte Lucas, who is willing to settle for Mr Collins.

In contrast to Daisy, Nick Carraway admires the imaginative qualities, which have allowed Gatsby to conceive of a life, better and finer than the one he was born into. But somehow in Nick's view, the life of New York, of the East, has corrupted and distorted Gatsby's vision. Daisy has not been able to match Gatsby's romantic idea of her, and the only means available to him to gain the wealth to sustain his conception of how life might be lived have been those provided by Wolfshiem, the adept manipulator of shady deals. Nick admires Gatsby to the end: in the closing paragraphs of the novel, he compares him to those who first saw America as a New World of unrealised human hopes. However often the hopes are disappointed, it is essential that hopefulness should be honoured as a fresh and unpolluted source of human energy, which might one day realise its dream.

Because of his belief that Gatsby has been corrupted and betrayed by New York, Nick Carraway leaves the East coast to return to the 'fundamental decencies' of the West. Fitzgerald does not explain this decision, nor does he make explicit, what these fundamental decencies are. The references to the Mid-West and to the 'solid rock' upon which human behaviour might be grounded, taken along with the Biblical associations of that phrase, might suggest that he is returning to a more primitive, if more conventional, way of life, rooted in 'self-disciplined Christian belief of a fundamentalist kind'. But no explicit statement of this kind can be found in the novel. In any case, the main impression left on the reader is Nick Carraway's belief in the value of Gatsby's capacity for wonder, which is not diminished by the tawdriness of his dream's realisation.

The Great Gatsby is a much more puzzling novel than *Pride and Prejudice*, but both novels demand careful reading. Jane Austen's book demonstrates that there is a considerable difference between the events of the story (which we may think of as raw material) and the novel as a finished work of art. The art of the novelist lies in his or her treatment of this raw material. As we have seen, the action of *Pride and Prejudice* begins at a rather arbitrary point in the sequence of events with which the novel deals. Only as it unfolds are we shown the episodes in the past which help to make intelligible the actions and attitudes of the characters in the present time of the novel.

But in *Pride and Prejudice* the revelation of the past implies a sense of completion. The unravelling of the past brings with it a sense of order, a pattern which can be grasped by the reader. *The Great Gatsby* shares this design to some extent. The past history of Gatsby is very gradually revealed to the reader through the accounts (which sometimes contradict one another) of Gatsby himself, as well as through the reminiscences of Wolfshiem and of Gatsby's father. We finish the novel with a clear knowledge of Gatsby's history. But some readers may well find it difficult to know where their sympathies lie. Are we to share Nick Carraway's veneration (the word is not too strong) for Gatsby's devotion to his ideal? This question is really a double one – does Fitzgerald mean us to share it? And can we share it?

These are questions which take us beyond the subject of this chapter. A careful look at these two novels has shown us that the novel and story are distinct concepts. But we have noticed that Fitzgerald uses techniques unfamiliar to Jane Austen. His use of 'West' and 'East' is a shorthand way of indicating meaning which Jane Austen does not use. His use of the notion of 'rock' is also something rather different. We can also point to his descriptions of the unsalubrious, ashy suburb of New York, where Wilson has his garage, as fixed in the same way. The 'valley of ashes' described in Chapter Two has a significance beyond its literal meaning; so too does the advertisement on which can be seen the blue and gigantic eyes of Dr J. T. Eckleburg. In these examples Fitzgerald is using means of expression which go beyond the literal presentation of things as they are, or might be. His 'valley of ashes' is akin to Bunyan's Slough of Despond, or City of Destruction: the literal description is stretched to cover the moral and spiritual state of the people who find themselves in these places. The eyes of J. T. Eckleburg have no such obviously applicable significance: to Wilson, they are the eyes of God, but it is not clear whether we are to believe him. In Chapter Seven Daisy sees a resemblance between the eyes of the advertisement and the eyes of Jay Gatsby. Fitzgerald leaves the reader to decide just what these references mean. Here he is using an expression, or motif, or figure in a much less direct way. 'Valley of ashes' is an expression with a single, clear and definite meaning of a non-literal kind: we may call it allegorical. We can see that in planning his novel, Fitzgerald has drawn to some extent on the allegorical tradition which, as we have seen in an earlier chapter, was one of the literary sources upon which novelists might draw. 'The eyes of J. T. Eckleburg' is as resonant an expression, but what it expresses is private to Fitzgerald and much less easy to pin down: in its original appearance in Chapter Two, it might be taken to refer to the indifference of a hypothetical god to the squalid world he has created; when associated with Gatsby's idealism, it might suggest an imaginative impulse which is not quenched by the depressing realities of the world as it is. Such an expression is capable of more than one use: it is multivalent, or ambiguous. To distinguish it from the other type of non-literal expression, we may call it 'symbolic', or 'a symbol'.

Observant readers may notice how Fitzgerald allows a perfectly literal adjective – the word 'green' – to develop non-literal significance during the course of the novel. There are about fourteen occurrences of this word, four of them in the closing pages of the novel; most of them are associated with Gatsby himself. Fitzgerald has enabled this simple word for a certain colour to pick up the meanings of freshness, innocence and energy which it may have in other contexts. The green light which draws Gatsby's attention to Daisy's house across the water in East Egg becomes an apt symbol for his power to imagine a quality of life beyond anything he has actually experienced.

A study of these two novels, then, has begun to open up for us an understanding of some of the techniques which the novelist may use to shape his material and to guide the interpretation which the reader must make of what he reads. Our study of *The Great Gatsby*, however, has shown that many puzzling questions of interpretation may remain, where the novelist has not chosen to be explicit, or where there is some ambiguity about his own interpretation of the material he has chosen to fashion into the form of fiction.

6 *The English Novel: Makers and Masters*

In the preceding chapters we have considered some of the ways in which novelists shape their novels; in this chapter we shall consider some of these changes in the perspective of history. In the course of the last two centuries — let us say roughly from the time of Scott and Jane Austen to the present — the practice of the novelist has moved between two fictional poles: some novelists have been attracted by the possibility of creating in their novels an image of the world as they knew it; others have been aware that their novels drew primarily on materials which existed only in their imagination. Perhaps, in general, we might say that the predominant strain in novels written in English in the nineteenth century was 'realistic'. The world of the novel, it was assumed, shared a border with the world in which everyday English men and women fell in love, married, and went about their trade and business. Contemporary readers of the fiction of Anthony Trollope (1815–82), or even of Jane Austen, might find little difference between the events of their novels and the events of their own lives. The predominant strain in American fiction during the same period was more purely imaginative: it opened up regions of the spirit which were more unusual, more extreme, and more alarming than the middle ground of English fiction. To make such a wide generalisation is to think immediately of exceptions; Charlotte and Emily Brontë may spring to mind, and so, of course, might Charles Dickens. But most readers would have agreed with the American novelist Nathaniel Hawthorne (1804– 64) when he defined the novel as a form which 'is presumed to aim at a very minute fidelity, not merely to the possible, but to the probable and ordinary course of man's experience'. Since the death of George Eliot (1819–80), however, fewer and fewer English novelists have aimed at this kind of realism: artists have ceased to believe in a common world of habit and convention which might be shared by all. They have been more aware of the variety of human experience; they have aimed above all at the truth of individual impression, at the singular vision or the special case.

During this time, attitudes to language itself have changed: it is no longer seen as a means of conveying factual knowledge or of truly depicting the world as it is. Students of language and of human psychology have pointed out that people use language to effect other purposes – to influence and persuade, to conceal or distort wishes they do not care to acknowledge to others or to themselves. It may be used as a weapon to destroy our enemies, or as a net to entrap them. Those who study language, or objects made of language – poems, novels, political speeches or historical documents – have become very sensitive to the subtle uses to which words may be put. From beginning to end, a novel is linguistic. Sentence by sentence, paragraph by paragraph we are challenged to understand the implications of individual words, of the grammatical patterns which link them together and of the extraordinary range of associations which words can gather round them. Distinctions of many kinds are expressed or implied by language: words can carry with them suggestions of social status; they may have historical, political or religious overtones. Ways of speech may suggest traits of character – superiority or grossness, sensitivity or boorishness.

It is often easy to fail to notice implications of this kind. Language, we tend to assume, simply refers to matters which are not linguistic. Of course, language *does* refer to a world beyond itself – to people, institutions, countries, ways of living and habits of thought which are quite independent of what might be said of them. So, we might say, the manners and customs referred to in *Pride and Prejudice* really did exist at the beginning of the nineteenth century in parts of England. Jane Austen was writing out of her own observation and experience. Her novels are valuable as a record of lives of the people she knew. In a sense, it may be said, novels are histories. Although there may be some truth in this view, a novel can tell us only partially and indirectly about 'real life'. The real life of a novel lies within the covers of the book where its words are printed. It lies in the structure, the design, the action, the characters and the setting of the novel.

These must be realised in the language and narrative techniques which the author has used. The substance of the novel – the material which has to be interpreted if the novel is to be understood – goes beyond what its characters do or say. As we have seen, it is easy to reduce the material of a novel to its 'story', to its paraphrasable content, but a summary of 'what happens' in the novel reduces, rather than explains, its meaning. The real substance of the novel lies in the patterns of meaning which can be found in its language.

Changes in attitudes to the function of language have helped to break the link between the novelist's imaginary world and the world of fact and history; they have also helped to alter the way modern readers approach the fiction of the past. If we recall the imagined setting of *Pride and Prejudice* or of *Emma*, it is remarkable how selective a picture Jane Austen gives us of the towns and villages in which the action of her novels takes place. Essentially her interest in large country houses, in Assembly rooms, in garrison towns or in country vicarages lies in what scope they will afford for human action. Readers of *Northanger Abbey* will not find much description of late-eighteenth-century Bath, though much of the novel is set there. It is, perhaps, the business of the historian to produce an account which describes and interprets the world as it has been; the novelist is free to select, to simplify, to exaggerate, to present a fictional world which does not *correspond* to the real world, but which may make some comment upon it. The novelist does not, in Hamlet's famous phrase, 'hold a mirror up to Nature': his aim is persuasive, even, possibly, propagandist. He wishes to persuade us to see the world as he sees it — freshly, unexpectedly. His delivery is oblique, unconventional, arresting; like the expert tennis-player, he serves with plenty of top-spin. What he delivers are special ways of using language which may persuade us to see human behaviour — including our own — in a new way. The reader who wants to improve his skill in reading must keep his eye on language, as a ball-game player keeps his eye on the ball. New language and new ways of seeing go together.

If we want to single out one figure in the history of nineteenth-century fiction who altered our expectations of what a novel might be like, we must choose Charles Dickens. His influence upon the English novel was profound and far more wide-reaching than the adjective 'Dickensian', applied to idiosyncratic character-types nearer to caricature than to real life, would suggest. His novels have a scope which goes beyond the study of the behaviour of individuals; the techniques he uses depend on the rhetorical effects of the preacher, the poet and the propagandist. They can be subtle, but for the most part they offer a broad vision of the nature of English society as Dickens experienced it. They translate into the characters and action of a novel generalisations about what it was like to live in the counties of England which Dickens knew best — and especially, of course, what it was like to live in London. The organisation of life in these places had produced environments which in turn produced human beings whose capacities and potentialities had been limited by the physical environments in which they had been brought up and by the institutions, creeds, prejudices, and assumptions which had created the circumstances in which they lived. The variety and diversity of attitudes and beliefs – the coexistence of benevolence and greed, of the vested interests of the established social classes and of the determination of gifted individuals to find a position in society for themselves – produced a social scene of equal variety. Dickens tried to grasp the whole of his society, to display its extraordinary social diversity as a single organism whose good and evil aspects could not easily be disentangled. If the modern reader sometimes feels irked by the narrowness of the social range of Jane Austen or George Eliot, it would be difficult to accuse Dickens of neglecting the contradictions and injustices of the society of his time. But his ambitious social range presented him with a technical problem.

Jane Austen's desire to trace with complete fidelity the consequences of the moral choices of her characters forced her to narrow her range: Dickens's desire to encompass the widest possible social range forced him to deal with action and character in new and different ways. Jane Austen brings the action of her characters to the test of clear moral principles: by the end of her novels the results of her characters' actions clearly show us what kind of behaviour we are to admire and what we are to reject. But Dickens's gifts as a novelist do not lie in such minute moral analysis. In his novel, *Bleak House* (1853), for example, a central group of characters (Richard Carstone and Esther Summerson, in particular) are allowed to make choices, form judgements and act in ways which have significant consequences for their lives; but other characters exist, not to behave well or badly, to make well- or ill-advised choices, but to demonstrate or illustrate kinds of behaviour which Dickens presents as admirable, ridiculous or disgraceful. Such characters have a representative function; they are types which their society has created. Thus Mrs Pardiggle and Mrs Jellyby represent types of charitable ladies whose interest in the well-being of strangers prevents them attending to their duties at home. Mr Vholes, the lawyer who sponges on Richard Carstone, is a personification of greed; Jo, the crossing-sweeper, is the innocent victim of a neglectful society. Such characters remind us of the people in Bunyan's *Pilgrim's Progress*, whose nature is defined by their names: they are animated virtues and vices, whose actions are predetermined by their characters.

Other characters in the novel exist for more complex purposes. Krook, the keeper of the rag-and-bone shop, is a mirror-image of the Lord Chancellor in whose Court of Chancery the law suit of Jarndyce *v.* Jarndyce, which drags its slow way through the novel, is being argued out. By means of Krook, Dickens is able to suggest the foul underside of legal practice which he believed was hidden by the impressive splendour of the English legal system. When Krook disintegrates in a mysterious explosion, which Dickens describes as 'spontaneous combustion', it is difficult for the reader to believe in this occurrence as a matter of fact, but this does not affect the force of the episode as a symbolic representation of how things which are rotten and unsound may collapse because they are past redemption and impossible to reform. A character of this sort helps the author to give vivid life to his own judgement about a complex human institution. Other characters, and much of the action, support Dickens's view about the corruption of some aspects of the law in his day.

The difference between, say, *Emma* and *Bleak House* is that the first is an *example* of human behaviour, worked out in specific detail with close attention to the effects of the actions of characters upon each other. Jane Austen is also interested in exploring the different ways characters perceive themselves and their companions; she enjoys studying the complexity of the small piece of society which she has made her own. In Dickens's novels we are presented with a powerfully argued case which seeks to provide a comprehensive, unified account of social relationships that does not depend upon close analysis of particular examples. The reader must also recognise that Dickens does not rely on argument and demonstration but on powerful rhetorical skills which use laughter, suspense, sympathy and pathos to persuade us to see things in his way. In Dickens's novels normal human functioning has been distorted by the unnatural circumstances in which most human beings have been nurtured. Hence his characters are for the most part eccentric, gnarled, grotesque. Now and then, as if by miracle, one or two people escape the domination of circumstances: in *Bleak House* Esther Summerson grows up unaffected by the unloving upbringing she has received from her foster-mother; Jo, the crossing-sweeper, has been nourished by the very few acts of human kindness which he has received during his life of material deprivation and of spiritual and intellectual ignorance; George Rouncewell, the keeper of the shooting gallery, and his friends, the Bagnets, have retained a simple neighbourliness and sense of friendship more typical of the manners of the countryside than of the alienating streets of the city.

The action in which these characters, good and bad, take part is in itself a parable. The long process of the law-suit ends in futility, the disputed estate swallowed up in legal costs. The search for Lady Dedlock, whose irregular relationship with a rakish young army captain had led to the birth of Esther Summerson, ends when she is discovered at the pauper's grave of her lover, dressed in the clothes of a working-class woman whom Esther had befriended. Family secrets are brought to light; estranged relationships are reconciled. Out of the squalor and decay of the phantasmagoric London of the novel order and harmony have been produced. *Bleak House* is a complex metaphor for the state of English society as Dickens saw it. As an instrument of reform, the book could only have been successful if it had correctly drawn attention to abuses which should have been put right. Many novels in the past have been books of this kind; having fulfilled their function, they have dropped out of sight. But *Bleak House* has survived to be read and enjoyed for its own sake. As a work of art, its power lies in the coherence of its design – not in its truth to fact but in its consistency, in the intrinsic power of the fable, and of the rhetoric which supports it, to convince us of the message it contains, that Mercy is to be preferred to Justice, Love to Revenge. Perhaps in the end, we may think, *Bleak House* was never intended to be an *analysis* of the ills of any society; it is a kind of magic ritual which, by producing light out of darkness, strengthens the capacity of its readers to do the same.

In his later novels Dickens makes powerful use of the ability of people and places to represent concepts which have a wider significance than they have in themselves. Prisons in *Little Dorrit* (1857) suggest psychological and social barriers to free self-development as well as the literal prison where Mr Dorrit and his family spend so much of their lives; the dust heaps in *Our Mutual Friend* (1865), from which Mr Boffin derives his fortune, suggest the tainted nature of the commercial civilisation of Dickens's time; the river Thames in the same novel becomes a symbol for the squalor and degradation of the city. Perhaps Dickens can be said to have freed the English novel from the tyranny of the probable. His novels deflected the reader's attention from too narrow a preoccupation with psychological and moral questions to wider issues concerning the nature of society and the kind of excellences which it fostered. His methods of writing employ a dazzling range of linguistic devices; above all he stresses the role of metaphor and analogy in helping us to think about complex issues. The design of his novels, sometimes consciously modelled on parables from the New Testament, serve as recommendations about how social organisations might be improved; their characters and settings represent simplifications of the complex facts and circumstances of real life upon which his recommendations were based. If men like Krook or Vholes, or families like the Smallweeds existed, if places like Tom-All-Alone's could stand for large areas of London, something must be done to change them and to change the hearts of the people who permitted them to continue.

No attempt has been made here to examine in detail the rhetorical means which Dickens used to attain his ends. It is enough to have suggested the new directions which his innovations allowed the English novel to take. He enlarged its scope; he extended the range of the material it might include; he used the materials of popular fiction and of family entertainment to discuss themes of national significance. Like Shakespeare in his history plays, he united consideration of the gravest matters of state with vivid representations of the ordinary life of a wide variety of social types, who displayed the impulses, passions and desires which required communal organisation, accommodation, regulation and satisfaction.

Later novelists, English and European, profited from his example. The modern novel in English, whether from Britain or America, or from English-speaking countries of the Commonwealth or elsewhere, has been influenced by his use in his novels of the imaginative and the fantastic. Following his example, later novelists did not hesitate to break the limits which discursive prose seemed to set on the way we see the world. The language of the novelist might be as resourceful as the language of the poet: after Dickens, the novelist no longer needed to think of himself as a historian of the external; now he was more closely attuned to the inner worlds of personal experience and individual vision. In later generations novelists became more and more aware of the extent of the territory of the inner life which remained for them to explore.

One of the most significant of the following generation of English novelists, Thomas Hardy (1840–1928), who began to publish his novels a year or two after the death of Charles Dickens, extended still further the use of poetic technique in the structure of his novels. In setting, Hardy's novels are as far as they can be from those of Dickens. His subject-matter is the countryside and its people, but their life provides him with a no less powerful metaphor for the condition of England than did city life for Dickens. Hardy, however, gives far more space to argument and speculation; parts of his novels are more abstract and theoretical; they are also less unified. Hardy's techniques suggest the interplay of many voices: argument and abstract speculation may suggest one set of approaches to the action of his novels. Often indeed this 'voice' in the novel has all the authority of the narrator himself; but the words and actions of the characters may throw a different light on their situation, while yet another approach may be suggested by the patterns of imagery which can be traced through the language of the novel. All of these voices may have an implicit or explicit commentary to make on Hardy's themes, and the novel may be reduced in significance if the reader allows only one of them to be heard. Special tact is needed not to rush to judgements which see only one side of the debate: Hardy's novels are a test of the reader's capacity to suspend judgement, to be alive to nuances of meaning, or ambiguities, and to tolerate contradictions.

As we move into the twentieth century we must become more aware of the danger of associating the author too firmly with any one of the sources of interpretation of his book. Less and less can the reader rely on firm guidance about interpretation: the actions of the characters in modern novels may be difficult to understand. There may be no commentary by a narrator, or the comments may be oblique and indirect, or even misleading: the burden of interpretation rests on the reader. It would be wrong to overemphasise the 'modernity' of the growth of a certain distance between author and reader. Irony, and the withholding of information from the reader, had long been ways of disguising the novelists' intentions. In *Vanity Fair* (1848) Thackeray uses a style of narration which teases the reader into repeated acts of judgement about behaviour which the narrator has ironically commended or described as normal. In *Emma* (1814) Jane Austen's ironic narrative style constantly invites the reader to judge the difference between Emma's estimate of herself and the real moral worth of her behaviour. Throughout the series of novels which she wrote between *Adam Bede* in 1859 and *Daniel Deronda* in 1876, George Eliot turns an increasingly sardonic glance upon characters whose behaviour seems questionable or insincere. But nineteenth-century novelists rarely, if ever, left their ironies, or their mysteries, unresolved: their novels were designed to clarify what was uncertain, to point directly to worthwhile standards and values. Admired twentieth-century authors (Conrad, Joyce, E. M. Forster, Virginia Woolf, for example) are more elusive; they are content to leave their novels open-ended. The tone of voice in which their narrators address the reader or comment on the action of the novel is impersonal, non-committal, or wayward, ironic, mocking, ambivalent. Thomas Hardy has the merit of standing between these traditions. In the chapter that follows we shall look in close detail at the methods he has used to design one of his finest novels.

7 Pattern and Design in the Structure of the Novel: A Study of Tess of the d'Urbervilles

A close study of how Hardy has shaped the narrative of *Tess of the d'Urbervilles* (1891) will allow us to bring together many of the ideas considered separately in other chapters of this book. Hardy's novel has a narrator who comments freely on the action. His novel is apparently conventional enough: it tells a story, it displays characters in action, it has a paraphrasable 'plot' which may be linked to tragedy or to those more naive ballad tales of simple country girls who come to grief because of some misfortune in their lives. What closer study will show is that Hardy's design is more complex than has so far been suggested and that the apparent simplicity of the story is qualified by the contrasting elements of the overall pattern which Hardy has devised for his novel. Let us begin by presenting, in summary form, what might appear to be 'the story' of the novel.

Tess of the d'Urbervilles is divided into seven sections or 'phases', as Hardy calls them. Tess Durbeyfield, an innocent country girl, is persuaded to visit a rich family who are believed by her parents to be distant relatives. Alec d'Urberville, her supposed cousin, arranges for her to work as a poultry girl, and then seduces her. She returns home to have her baby, but it dies, and some years later she leaves home to work as a dairy maid on a distant farm. There, she meets Angel Clare, the son of a clergyman, who long before had seen her briefly as he passed through her village: they fall in love, and without knowing anything of Tess's previous history, Clare offers to marry her, and, with some reluctance, she accepts him. When she tells him of her past on their wedding night, he decides that they must part. Angel goes to Brazil, while Tess goes back after a time to work on a farm. After an unsuccessful attempt to make contact with Clare's parents, she chances to meet her seducer, Alec d'Urberville, now reformed and converted into a way-side preacher. He offers to marry her, and abandons his preaching to follow her. In desperation she writes to Clare, but, hearing nothing from him and worn out with her work on the farm and distressed by the hardships that follow her father's death, she is eventually won back to Alec. When Clare finally returns home he finds her living with Alec in lodgings in a seaside town on the south coast of England. Ashamed at having given way to Alec's persuasiveness, full of remorse for having despaired of her husband, she murders Alec with a carving knife and follows Clare. For some days they live together in an empty house in the country; disturbed, they take to the road again, and are found at the ancient monument, Stonehenge, by policemen who arrest Tess. For the murder of Alec d'Urberville, she is hanged.

Such a summary of the action of the novel tells us nothing about its quality, or about its meaning. It conveys nothing of the experience of reading the novel or what might be gained by the experience. As students of the novel, our task is to attempt to analyse its qualities so that we have a firmer grasp of what makes reading it worthwhile. How, then, can we describe it so that more of its characteristic features can be brought to our attention?

Perhaps one way to begin is to consider the sections, or phases into which the novel is divided. Hardy uses the word 'phase' to describe the stages of Tess's life; it is a word we would normally associate with the waxing and waning of the moon from its first appearance as a slender crescent to fullness and then to its broken, pitted appearance as it comes to the end of its cycle: traditionally, these phases of the moon have been associated with the major stages of the life of a woman — maiden, wife, old woman. The first two phases of Hardy's novel, 'The Maiden', and 'Maiden No More' represent the first stage of Tess's life; the next three, 'The Rally', 'The Consequence' and 'The Woman Pays' represent the second and the last two, 'The Convert' and 'Fulfilment' represent her decline. Perhaps we may see the novel as a picture with three panels: the first represents Tess's experiences with Alec d'Urberville, the second presents her meeting with Angel Clare, the third returns her to Alec, until Clare comes to claim her and Alec is killed. Of these three sections, the third is the shortest, though many events take place in it; the first has the nature of a prelude, though what happens in it forms the first completed cycle of Tess's life. It is in the second section that the core of the novel lies, and its three sections again complete a cycle, self-contained, but an intelligible consequence of the first section of the book. The first cycle of the novel begins in May and ends in August; the second begins in May, reaches its climax at the turning of the year and ends the following winter; the third section reaches its conclusion in the Spring of the next year. This is the bare framework on which Hardy stretches his canvas.

Clearly, one of the principles which Hardy has used in designing his novel is the principle of contrast: Alec and Clare are contrasted types of men. Tess moves from Alec to Angel back to Alec, then back to Angel. Indeed, Hardy brings Angel Clare into the narrative right at the beginning of the novel, where he has a first glimpse of Tess: so Tess's alternation between the men has a perfect symmetry: Clare − Alec − Clare − Alec − Clare. Hardy's narrator has no doubt that part of Tess's misfortune lay in the fact that she and Angel failed to meet at the first occasion they might have done so. But things are not so well ordered as they might be in this human world where chance seems predominant. Here are the narrator's reflections after Tess has met Alec d'Urberville − the wrong man − for the first time.

> Thus the thing began. Had [Tess] perceived this meeting's import she might have asked why she was doomed to be seen and coveted that day by the wrong man, and not by some other man, the right and desired one in all respects − as nearly as humanity can supply the right and desired; yet to him who amongst her acquaintance might have approximated to this kind, she was but a transient impression, half forgotten.
>
> In the ill-judged execution of the well-judged plan of things the call seldom produces the comer, the man to love rarely coincides with the hour for loving. Nature does not often say 'See!' to her poor creature at a time when seeing can lead to happy doing; or reply 'Here' to a body's cry of 'Where?' till the hide-and-seek has become an irksome, outworn game. We may wonder whether at the acme and summit of the human progress these anachronisms will be corrected by a finer intuition, a closer interaction of the social machinery than that which now jolts us round and along; but such completeness is not to be prophesied, or even conceived as possible. Enough that in the present case, as in millions, it was not the two halves of a perfect whole that confronted each other at the perfect moment; a missing counterpart wandered independently about the earth waiting in crass obtuseness till the late time came. Out of which maladroit delay sprang anxieties, disappointments, shocks, catastrophes, and passing-strange destinies.[1]

This is not untypical of the kind of commentary which the narrative voice of the novel offers the reader. How is it to be interpreted? Notice how the commentary begins close to Tess herself. The second sentence of the first paragraph claims to tell us what Tess's thoughts might have been, if she could have foreseen her fate. But the word 'doom' is not the narrator's; it is how he thinks Tess might have judged her life. Notice how ambiguous the tone of the narrator's commentary is – 'the right and desired one in all respects – as nearly as humanity can supply the right and desired'. The qualification so undercuts the object of Tess's fancy, that we wonder whether it could ever be more than an illusion. The tone of the writing is bleakly ironic. Tess is imagined to be thinking of the image of Angel Clare whom she had seen once, and whose memory she cherished: to Angel she has been 'a transient impression'. When the narrator moves away from Tess, to speak more directly to the reader his tone becomes more mordantly pessimistic. To whom are we to attribute 'the well-judged plan of things'? Is this another human illusion which can only be saved by the proviso that it is never satisfactorily carried out? How is the reader to judge whether sarcasm or sympathy predominates here? When the narrator speaks of 'the acme and summit of the human progress' do we consider that he believes in the possibility of human perfectibility, or is this yet another human illusion which he mentions only to dismiss? Sarcasm would be the wrong word for the narrator's tone but surely it is right to say that it conveys a mixture of sympathy for the human lot with some impatience for the weakness of human expectations. The narrator contrasts known reality with an ideal which may be desired but which more clear-sighted creatures would know could never be attained. The 'crass obtuseness' in which 'the counterpart' – the heart's desire – wanders is surely the cloud of ignorance by which human life is surrounded.

Even this brief examination of two paragraphs from the novel is sufficient to show that *Tess of the d'Urbervilles* is no simple tale. The tone of this novel is not easy to pin down: it is sad, ironic, impatient of, yet sympathetic to, human weakness. The commentary on the novel addresses itself to an audience which is educated, reflective, interested in the strangeness of human experience, and which has a breadth of mind far greater than that shown by any of the characters in the novel. Unlike the characters, the voice of the narrative is self-conscious, acutely aware of irony and paradox: it is only through a sympathetic understanding of the commentary that the reader can begin to appreciate the depth of human understanding which is reached by

Hardy in this novel.

The narrative voice is only one of the techniques which Hardy uses to guide the reader's response. Consider how he uses place and season to arrange the pattern of his novel: Tess and her family live in a village in the Vale of Blackmore, which Hardy describes as quite different in character from Talbothays in the Valley of the Great Dairies, where she meets Angel Clare and spends the summer of pleasure and warmth which leads to her marriage. Both these places are quite different from the farm at Flintcomb Ash where she spends the winter, abandoned by Clare and not yet rediscovered by Alec d'Urberville. These three places constitute the principal settings of *Tess of the d'Urbervilles.* Each setting supports the mood of the action which takes place there. Hardy's descriptions of place may seem uninspired and clumsy, but during the course of the novel the reader comes to know the tract of country he called Wessex, so that we begin to sympathise with Hardy's feeling for place and with his characters' experience of the demands that close contact with the countryside can make on human and animal endurance. Compare Hardy's first description of the place where Tess was born with the places to which her later adventures bring her. This description of her home village appears in the second chapter of the novel:

The village of Marlott lay amid the north-eastern undulations of the beautiful Vale of Blakemore or Blackmoor ... an engirdled and secluded region, for the most part untrodden as yet by tourist or landscape-painter, though within a few hours' journey from London. ...

This fertile and sheltered tract of country, in which the fields are never brown and the springs never dry, is bounded on the south by the bold chalk ridge that embraces the prominences of Hambledon Hill, Bulbarrow, Nettlecombe-Tout, Dogbury, High Stoy and Bubb Down. The traveller from the coast, who, after plodding northward for a score of miles over calcareous downs and corn-lands, suddenly reaches the verge of one of these escarpments, is surprised and delighted to behold, extended like a map beneath him, a country differing absolutely from that which he has passed through. Behind him the hills are open, the sun blazes down upon the fields so large as to give an unenclosed character to the land-scape, the lanes are white, the hedges low and plashed, the atmosphere colourless. Here, in the valley, the world seems to be constructed upon a smaller and more delicate scale; the fields are mere paddocks, so reduced that from this height their hedgerows appear a network of dark green threads overspreading the paler green of the grass. The atmosphere beneath is languorous, and is so tinged with azure that what artists call the middle distance partakes also of that hue, while the horizon beyond is of the deepest ultramarine. Arable lands are few and limited; with but slight exceptions the prospect is a broad rich mass of grass and trees, mantling minor hills and dales within the major. Such is the Vale of Blackmoor.[2]

This introduction to the geography of the novel may seem too much like a guide-book in style, but in fact it contains details which are valuable for an understanding of the novel. The north–south axis upon which Hardy's description rests is significant as a bird's-eye view of Tess's future wanderings. The difference in character between Marlott and the country to the south is moral as well as geographical. The landscape varies from small-scale to large as Tess moves from innocence to experience. Here is how Hardy marks the contrast between the Vale of Blackmoor and Talbothays, the farm in the Valley of the Great Dairies, where the central action of the novel takes place:

It was intrinsically different from the Vale of Little Dairies, Blackmoor Vale, which, save during her disastrous sojourn at Trantridge, she had exclusively known till now. The world was drawn to a larger pattern here. The enclosures numbered fifty acres instead of ten, the farmsteads were more extended, the groups of cattle formed tribes hereabout; there only families. These myriads of cows stretching under her eyes from the far east to the far west outnumbered any she had ever seen at one glance before. . . . The bird's eye perspective before her was not so luxuriantly beautiful, perhaps, as that other one which she knew so well; yet it was more cheering. It lacked the intensely blue atmosphere of the rival vale, and its heavy soils and scents; the new air was clear, bracing, ethereal. The river itself, which nourished the grass and cows of these renowned dairies, flowed not like the streams in Blackmoor. Those were slow, silent, often turbid; flowing over beds of mud into which the incautious wader might sink and vanish unawares. The Froom waters were clear as the pure River of Life shown to the Evangelist, rapid as the shadow of a cloud, with pebbly shallows that prattled to the sky all day long. There the water-flower was the lily; the crowfoot here.[3]

Talbothays presents a wider world than Marlott. In comparison with the Vale of the Great Dairies, the Vale of Blackmoor seems reduced, less attractive. And yet the reader's impression is tinged with doubt. The cattle in Talbothays are grouped in 'tribes' — a less homely and personal expression, one might think, than the 'families' of Marlott. The Vale of Blackmoor is portrayed as static, unchanging, beautiful; the waters of its river travel over thick mud of unfathomable depth. By contrast, the waters of the Vale of Froom are 'clear, bracing, ethereal'. But that last word, so often associated with Angel Clare, carries a hint of idealism, a distrust of the physical, which may make the reader doubtful what effect Hardy means to suggest. The waters of life, shown to the Evangelist in the Book of Revelation, flow through a celestial city of which it is said, 'And there shall in no wise enter into it anything that defileth, neither whatsoever worketh abomination, or maketh a lie: but they which are written in the Lamb's book of life.' Readers may doubt whether Hardy means us to believe that Tess would pass this test in the eyes of those who considered themselves pure. Even Tess herself, when a few paragraphs later she sings a hymn of praise to the Lord, stops and murmurs to herself, 'But perhaps I don't quite know the Lord yet.' The waters of the Froom are rapid, but 'rapid as the shadow of a cloud' and these 'pebbly shallows that prattled to the sky all day long' may seem superficial, transient, unthinkingly and unjustifiably glad. When Tess descends lower into the valley (where, we are told, it could only be 'read aright'), Tess finds that the river has lost its impetus and now seems 'exhausted, aged, and attenuated', rather, the context suggests, as 'the once powerful d'Urbervilles were now'. The symbol of the Valley of Blackmoor is the lily of purity; the symbol of the Valley of Froom is the crowfoot of experience and age. Looking closely at the detail of this passage we may believe that Hardy has endowed his description with hints of the sinister experiences which await Tess in this Valley that looks so fair.

When Tess finds herself on the valley's lower slopes, Hardy emphasises her sense of littleness:

Not quite sure of her direction Tess stood still upon the hemmed expanse of verdant flatness, like a fly on a billiard table of indefinite length, and of no more consequence to the surroundings than that fly.[4]

In Chapter Forty-three Hardy repeats the striking comparison he has drawn between Tess and the fly. By now she is working on a turnip field at Flintcomb Ash, one of the farms on the chalky downs and cornlands which overlook the Vale of Blackmoor and lie between the two valleys whose description we have been examining.

> ... the whole field was in colour a desolate drab; it was a complexion without features, as if a face, from chin to brow, should be only an expanse of skin. The sky wore, in another colour, the same likeness; a white vacuity of countenance with the lineaments gone. So these two upper and nether visages confronted each other all day long, the white face looking down on the brown face, and the brown face looking up at the white face, without anything standing between them but the two girls crawling over the surface of the former like flies.[5]

Hardy's description of this scene is horrifying and grotesque; we are reminded of the technique of surrealist painters or of the shocking transformation of the lifeless into a frightening parody of the living, which we might see in a science-fiction or horror film. Hardy's presentation of the third significant landscape in the novel is more explicit than either of the others, and yet it is clearly linked with them. Here is Tess approaching Flintcomb Ash:

> Towards the second evening she reached the irregular chalk table-land or plateau, bosomed with semi-globular tumuli – as if Cybele the Many-breasted were supinely extended there – which stretched between the valley of her birth and the valley of her love.
>
> Here the air was dry and cold, and the long cart-roads were blown white and dusty within a few hours after rain. There were few trees, or none, those that would have grown in the hedges being mercilessly plashed down with the quickset by the tenant-farmers, the natural enemies of tree, bush, and brake. . . . Before her, in a slight depression, were the remains of a village. She had, in fact, reached Flintcomb-Ash . . . . There seemed to be no help for it; hither she was doomed to come. The stubborn soil around her showed plainly enough that the kind of labour in demand here was of the roughest kind; but it was time to rest from searching . . . .[6]

It was from the viewpoint of this landscape that in Chapter Two Hardy first described to us the Vale of Blackmoor. The fields of Flintcomb Ash, he then told us, were 'so large as to give an unenclosed character to the landscape': now, in this more detailed description, we can appreciate the sense of abandonment which Tess feels there. The progressive extension of the size of the fields in each of the landscapes through which she moves reduces Tess to insignificance: the white lanes, the colourless atmosphere suggest the dryness and indifference of the landscape. The 'plashed' hedges are now shown to be examples of natural things 'mercilessly' bent to the will of the farmers, enemies of growth and luxuriance. This landscape, bosomed with semi-globular tumuli – 'as if Cybele the Many-breasted were supinely extended there' and littered (as Hardy tells us later) with 'loose white flints in bulbous cusped and phallic shapes' – is indifferent to the gentler human values which Tess represents, and which she had hoped Angel Clare would share with her. It is a high chalky plateau where are to be found remorseless labour, lust, cruelty and greed. Hardy sums up the effect of it on Tess as follows:

> Thus Tess walks on; a figure which is part of the landscape; a field-woman pure and simple, in winter guise, a gray serge cape, a red woollen cravat, a stuff skirt covered by a whitey-brown rough wrapper, and buff-leather gloves. Every thread of that old attire has become faded and thin under the stroke of raindrops, the burn of sunbeams, and the stress of winds. There is no sign of young passion in her now –
> The maiden's mouth is cold
>   . . .
> Fold over simple fold
> Binding her head.
> Inside this exterior, over which the eye might have roved as over a thing scarcely percipient, almost inorganic, there was the record of a pulsing life which had learnt too well, for its years, of the dust and ashes of things, of the cruelty of lust and the fragility of love.[7]

Just as landscape can occasionally come to life as some monstrous kind of human being, so humanity can be subdued to the earth into something without life or character. Tess's life as she approaches Flintcomb Ash has been reduced to a stage not far short of what she anticipated when, 'maiden no more', she began to think that one day she would be dead, 'grassed down and forgotten'.

These landscapes of *Tess of the d'Urbervilles* have a clear literary purpose; each provides the frame and background for the stages in Tess's life which take her farther and farther from the safe shelter of her home; they are external symbols of the interior experiences of her soul. But it is worth noticing that while Hardy clearly uses land-scape in the symbolic way described above, he is also at other times careful to separate living things from landscape. Again and again, he insists on the indifference of 'the world' to the human beings who live there. When Tess arrives at Talbothays, Hardy makes a point of stressing the indifference of the valley to her arrival. The episode in Chapter Four, referred to earlier on pages 43–4, can now be seen to have a significant place in the design of the novel as a whole. There Hardy describes Abraham as he

> leant back against the hives, and with upturned face made obser-vations on the stars, whose cold pulses were beating amid the black hollows above, in serene dissociation from these two wisps of human life. He asked how far away those twinklers were, and whether God was on the other side of them.[8]

Indifferent as the stars seem (Hardy stresses their indifference in phrases such as 'cold pulses' and 'serene dissociation'), they offer an irresistible temptation to human beings, who believe that in some way their fates are attached to the larger movements of the world. From ancient times men have looked up to the stars believing that they influenced their lives for good or evil. Thus, after Abraham has fallen asleep beside her:

> with no longer a companion to distract her, Tess fell more deeply into reverie than ever, her back leaning against the hives. The mute procession past her shoulders of trees and hedges became attached to fantastic scenes outside reality, and the occasional heave of the wind became the sign of some immense sad soul, conterminous with the universe in space, and with history in time.[9]

These thoughts are attributed to Tess – they are not the commentary of the narrator. We are being told what Tess thinks; the narrator does not suggest that what she thinks is true. Indeed, here we may find some clue which will help us to explain the apparently inevitable movement downwards, as Tess makes her way through the landscapes which Hardy has prepared for her. Reverie and illusion are aspects of Tess's character which contribute to her downfall. They are in Hardy's view fundamental flaws which are to be found in most human thinking: most human life is founded upon illusion. Think of the dreams which warm life for Tess's father and mother as they escape from the 'muck and muddle of rearing children'. In Chapter Three, Hardy has this to say of Mrs Durbeyfield's visits to the local inn:

> To discover him at Rolliver's, to sit there for an hour or two by his side and dismiss all thought and care of the children during the interval made her happy. A sort of halo, an occidental glow, came over life then. Troubles and other realities took on themselves a metaphysical impalpability, sinking to mere mental phenomena for serene contemplation, and no longer stood as pressing concretions which chafed body and soul. . . . She felt a little as she used to feel when she sat by her now wedded husband in the same spot during his wooing, shutting her eyes to his defects of character, and regarding him only in his ideal presentation as lover.[10]

Once again, it is worthwhile to attend carefully to Hardy's language, no matter how 'strange' or 'difficult' it may appear. Passages of this kind introduce us to material which goes far deeper than the carefully written descriptions of landscape which form appropriate backgrounds to the story of Tess. Here, we are being introduced to a far-reaching theme in the novel, which appears in many different forms. Notice that Hardy's commentary leaves much work for the reader to do. What judgement are we to make here of Mrs Durbeyfield? Is her escape from the cares of her life pardonable human weakness, or is it a much more serious error? What do we make of her willingness to 'dismiss all thought and care of the children'? Is it sensible to allow her problems and difficulties to become a kind of fantasy which she can contemplate with an undisturbed detachment? What will be the result of her 'shutting her eyes' to her husband's faults of character? Is life best seen through 'a sort of halo'?

'Ideal' and 'real' clash many times in this novel with consequences which may seem ominous. Think of the folk of Trantridge dancing together on their weekly visit to Chaseborough. As Hardy describes it, the village dance takes on a lurid, hallucinatory quality:

It was a windowless erection used for storage, and from the open door there floated into the obscurity a mist of yellow radiance, which at first Tess thought to be illuminated smoke. But on drawing nearer she perceived that it was a cloud of dust, lit by candles within the outhouse, whose beams upon the haze carried forward the outline of the doorway into the wide night of the garden.

When she came close and looked in she beheld indistinct forms racing up and down to the figure of the dance, the silence of their footfalls arising from their being overshoe in 'scroff' — that is to say, the powdery residuum from the storage of peat and other products, the stirring of which by their turbulent feet created the nebulosity that involved the scene. Through this floating, fusty debris of peat and hay, mixed with the perspirations and warmth of the dancers, and forming together a sort of vegeto-human pollen, the muted fiddles feebly pushed their notes, in marked contrast to the spirit with which the measure was trodden out. They coughed as they danced, and laughed as they coughed. Of the rushing couples there could barely be discerned more than the high lights — the indistinct-ness shaping them to satyrs clasping nymphs — a multiplicity of Pans whirling a multiplicity of Syrinxes; Lotis attempting to elude Priapus, and always failing.

At intervals a couple would approach the doorway for air, and the haze no longer veiling their features, the demigods resolved them-selves into the homely personalities of her own next-door neigh-bours.[11]

The keyword in this passage, perhaps, is 'nebulosity' — haziness, vagueness, cloudiness. The haze is composed of sweat and dust — 'a vegeto-human pollen', a phrase which suggests the sexual energy of the scene. This illuminated dust throws the outline of the doorway of the building on to the dark, in much the same way as it aggrandises the work-people into classical figures until their 'homely' natures are restored to them when they step out of the transforming haze. Hardy's description of the scene manages to combine the down-to-earth realism of a Dutch genre painting with the ideal presentation of human emotions we might find in a classical painting by Poussin. But his suggestion is clear: the picture of life offered by the art of Classicism (or its Renaissance imitators) is an illusion. Human life is meaner than men like to picture it. Hardy makes further use through the novel of symbols of this kind to suggest the capacity people have for self-distortion, or self-aggrandisement. In Chapter Ten, he goes out of his way to emphasise the false sense of unity with Nature which alcohol and the physical exhilaration of the dance give to the country folk. As Tess and her companions walk home, just before the altercation takes place from which Alec D'Urberville 'rescues' her:

> Tess soon perceived ... that the fresh night air was producing staggerings and serpentine courses among the men who had partaken too freely; some of the more careless women also were wandering in their gait – to wit, a dark virago, Car Darch, dubbed Queen of Spades, till lately a favourite of d'Urberville's; Nancy, her sister, nick-named the Queen of Diamonds; and the young married woman who had already tumbled down. Yet however terrestrial and lumpy their appearance just now to the mean unglamoured eye, to themselves the case was different. They followed the road with a sensation that they were soaring along in a supporting medium, possessed of original and profound thoughts, themselves and surrounding nature forming an organism of which all the parts harmoniously and joyously interpenetrated each other. They were as sublime as the moon and stars above them, and the moon and stars were as ardent as they.[12]

Here, perhaps, is as good an example as we could find of Hardy's capacity to sympathise and to distinguish. He can fully enter into the feelings of his characters, while setting a distance between them and his narrator, who might well be the 'mean unglamoured eye' who looks on. The tone of the narrator suggests there is no 'supporting medium' for human beings in an alien inorganic world, that there is no joyful unity between man and nature. Elsewhere Hardy explicitly repudiates Wordsworth's view that 'Nature's holy plan' had been spoiled by men themselves; rather it was an illusion, a regrettable by-product of human egotism, to believe that human life was intended to be happy, or in harmony with Nature. Now, as the party moves on:

> ... these children of the open air, whom even excess of alcohol could scarce injure permanently, betook themselves to the field-path; and as they went there moved onward with them, around the shadow of each one's head, a circle of opalized light, formed by the moon's rays upon the glistening sheet of dew. Each pedestrian could see no halo but his or her own, which never deserted the head-shadow, whatever its vulgar unsteadiness might be; but adhered to

it, and persistently beautified it; till the erratic motions seemed an inherent part of the irradiation, and the fumes of their breathing a component of the night's mist; and the spirit of the scene, and of the moonlight, and of Nature, seemed harmoniously to mingle with the spirit of wine.[13]

By now Hardy's reader must be attuned to the voice of this narrator, which seems to mix irony with elegy, as it muses on the illusion, the 'saving lie', as Ibsen would call it, that adds dignity and purpose to human life.

When we come to consider the central action of the novel, Angel Clare's wooing of Tess, these human frailties are clearly associated with Angel and with Tess herself, who both share a human incapacity to see things as they are in reality. They cannot avoid fantasy and illusion about themselves and each other. Hardy speaks about Tess in terms curiously similar to those he used about the country people in the extracts quoted above. When she arrives in the Valley of Froom to begin her work as a dairymaid, 'her hopes mingled with the sunrise in an ideal photosphere which surrounded her as she bounded along against the soft south wind. She heard a pleasant voice in every breeze, and in every bird's note seemed to lurk a joy.' The Oxford English Dictionary cites this passage from *Tess* to illustrate the meaning of the word 'photosphere' as 'a sphere or orb of light, radiance or glory'. Hardy qualified it with the adjective 'ideal' which in his usage most commonly is contrasted with 'real'. Alongside Hardy's use of the word, the OED gives its meaning as a term in astronomy where it means 'the luminous envelope of the sun, from which its light and heat radiate'. Perhaps Hardy had this scientific use of the work in mind, for it is surely implied that Tess's 'photosphere' is a radiance produced by her own mind. Hardy uses the word in a later passage when he is describing Tess's love for Clare:

Her affection for him was now the breath and life of Tess's being; it enveloped her as a photosphere, irradiated her into forgetfulness of her past sorrows, keeping back the gloomy spectres that would persist in their attempts to touch her – doubt, fear, moodiness, care, shame. She knew they were waiting like wolves just outside the circumscribing light, but she had long spells of power to keep them in hungry subjection there.[14]

It is difficult to avoid the conclusion that the photosphere that surrounds Tess as she arrives at Talbothays, and reappears as she feels drawn closer to Angel Clare, has close associations with the haloes that surround the heads of the drunken country people returning from their dance to Trantridge. Notice, too, how the word 'irradiate' is used in both passages: it is a word that suggests 'brightness' and 'illumination'. But Tess is 'irradiated into forgetfulness'. Just as in Chapter Ten we read of the transformation of the Trantridge people at their dance, so in Chapter Nineteen we see something of the same kind happening to Tess; it occurs in the well-known episode in which Tess hears Angel Clare playing on his harp and is drawn to his music:

It was a typical summer evening in June, the atmosphere being in such delicate equilibrium and so transmissive that inanimate objects seemed endowed with two or three senses, if not five. There was no distinction between the near and the far, and an auditor felt close to everything within the horizon. The soundlessness impressed her as a positive entity rather than as the mere negation of noise. It was broken by the strumming of strings.

Tess had heard these notes in the attic above her head. Dim, flattened, constrained by their confinement, they had never appealed to her as now, when they wandered in the still air with a stark quality like that of nudity. To speak absolutely, both instrument and execution were poor; but the relative is all, and as she listened Tess, like a fascinated bird, could not leave the spot. Far from leaving she drew up towards the performer, keeping behind the hedge that he might not guess her presence.

The outskirt of the garden in which Tess found herself had been left uncultivated for some years, and was now damp and rank with juicy grass which sent up mists of pollen at a touch; and with tall blooming weeds emitting offensive smells — weeds whose red and yellow and purple hues formed a polychrome as dazzling as that of cultivated flowers. She went stealthily as a cat through this profusion of growth, gathering cuckoo-spittle on her skirt, cracking snails that were underfoot, staining her hands with thistle-milk and slug-slime, and rubbing off upon her naked arms sticky blights which, though snow-white on the apple-tree trunks, made madder stains on her skin; thus she drew quite near to Clare, still unobserved of him.

Tess was conscious of neither time nor space. The exaltation which she had described as being producible at will by gazing at a star, came now without any determination of hers; she undulated upon the thin notes of the second-hand harp, and their harmonies passed like breezes through her, bringing tears into her eyes. The floating pollen seemed to be his notes made visible, and the dampness of the garden the weeping of the garden's sensibility. Though near nightfall, the rank-smelling weed-flowers glowed as if they would not close for intentness and the waves of colour mixed with the waves of sound.[15]

In this passage Hardy might be accused of simply falling into 'the pathetic fallacy' of using natural objects as reflectors of human states of mind in a rather simple way. Tennyson (1809–92) had done this in his poetry when he wrote of the flowers welcoming the heroine of his poem 'Maud' (1855):

> There has fallen a splendid tear
> From the passion-flower at the gate.
> She is coming, my dove, my dear;
> She is coming, my life, my fate;
> The red rose cries, 'She is near, she is near';
> And the white rose weeps, 'She is late';
> The larkspur listens, 'I hear, I hear';
> And the lily whispers, 'I wait'.[16]

Perhaps those famous lines are too obviously decorative; the feelings of the lover are projected on to the flowers, not because it makes good sense that they should be, but because it adds the colour and vividness associated with the flowers to the feelings of the lover. But Hardy's description is rather different: we must surely read it within the context of the passages we have already considered, where the relation of human beings to the world in which they live has already been discussed. Hardy has already shown us many times that men and women are especially prone to attribute their own feelings falsely to the natural world in which they live, that they have a strong wish to feel that their desires and actions are in harmony with its mysterious movements. In the passage quoted above the reader is given the clearest indication of the strength and seductiveness of this mistaken belief. This is no mere literary device: it is a persistent error of the human imagination.

The account of Tess's enticement by the sound of Angel's harp is complex and subtle. The word 'transmissive' gives the very atmosphere of the summer evening an appearance of human activity. Hardy does not explain how this quality of the air appears to endow inanimate objects with human sense. Closely attended to, what this paragraph says is extraordinary: the human and the non-human world share for a moment a common consciousness. The human listener has a heightened awareness of the natural world: lifeless things see, hear, talk and touch. Space is annihilated; silence is audible. In this world turned upside down, Tess is now a bird, now a cat stalking its prey. Appreciating Angel's music for the first time, she is specially aware of the sexual feelings conveyed by the sound. As she approaches him through the untamed garden, Hardy uses the names and characters of the wild flowers to suggest complex confusions of attraction and repulsion in smells, colours and secretions which have strong sexual associations. White fungi rub against her skin to produce crimson stains there. Now Tess considers herself free from the bonds of space and time; she is all spirit, responding to Angel's music as an Aeolian harp might react to the random movements of the wind. Now the sound of music seems to merge with the appearance of the flowers; in this confusion of the senses, individuals disappear to be replaced by a generalised impressionability which sweeps through the whole landscape, linking the animate and the inanimate in an acutely sensitive capacity for feeling. Hardy does not remind us at this point of the judgement he has made elsewhere about the delusiveness of this human belief that man and Nature can be at one: only the reference to 'the pollen' may call to the reader's mind the mistaken sense of self-aggrandisement which a similar dusty mixture leant to the dreams of the country folk at Trantridge.

When Tess and Clare meet in the morning at the dairy-house, Hardy continues to describe them in the kind of imagery we have already noticed. The pollen mists are replaced by the strange haze of the morning light which conceals as much as it reveals:

> Being so often – possibly not always by chance – the first two persons to get up at the dairy-house, they seemed to themselves the first persons up of all the world. In these early days of her residence here Tess did not skim, but went out of doors at once after rising where [Angel] was generally awaiting her. The spectral, half-compounded, aqueous light which pervaded the open mead, impressed them with a feeling of isolation, as if they were Adam and

Eve. . . . Whilst all the landscape was in neutral shade his companion's face, which was the focus of his eyes, rising above the mist stratum, seemed to have a sort of phosphorescence upon it. She looked ghostly, as if she were merely a soul at large. In reality her face, without appearing to do so, had caught the cold gleam of day from the north-east; his own face, though he did not think of it, wore the same aspect to her. . . . Then it would grow lighter, and her features would become simply feminine; they had changed from those of a divinity who could confer bliss to those of a being who craved it.[17]

Once again, Hardy emphasises the strange halo which confers an ideal perfection on Tess in Angel's eyes, and in hers on Angel. Like the Trantridge peasants in their dance, Angel and Tess are transformed into idealised figures – into Adam and Eve, or 'a divinity who could confer bliss', though the light of day returns them to their everyday selves. To one another they are mysterious, half-understood products of each other's imagination.

The attraction between Tess and Angel is obviously strong, but their concept of one another is based on an idealisation which is cruelly deceptive, since neither is fully aware of the mistake which is being made. Tess, however, is aware of a quite specific deception which she has practised on Clare: she knows she is not the virginal dairymaid he takes her to be. She thinks she means to tell him about her past before they are married. One attempt to do this – the letter which miscarries – fails by ill-luck; but at other times the failure lies in Tess's will. She knows that Angel is being strongly drawn to her, but she resists the idea that he might ask her to marry him. We are told that their relationship grows without their conscious knowledge: 'All the while they were converging, under an irresistible law, as surely as two streams in one vale.' (Chapter Twenty). When Angel holds Tess in his arms at the end of Chapter Twenty-four we read, 'Nobody had beheld the gravitation of the two into one.' Tess's attachment to Clare is not a matter of her will; it takes place beneath the level of understanding and conscious choice, and her later attempts to refuse him come to nothing. He cannot understand why they should not marry, and Tess is unable to prevent herself being carried along by the drift of events:

In reality, she was drifting into acquiescence. Every see-saw of her breath, every wave of her blood, every pulse singing in her ears, was a voice that joined with nature in revolt against her scrupulousness. Reckless, inconsiderate acceptance of him; to close with him at the altar, revealing nothing, and chancing discovery; to snatch ripe pleasure before the iron teeth of pain could have time to shut upon her: that was what love counselled; and in almost a terror of ecstasy Tess divined that, despite her many months of lonely self-chastise-ment, wrestlings, communings, schemes to lead a future of austere isolation, love's counsels would prevail.[18]

'Love' here is part of what elsewhere in the novel Hardy calls 'the instinctive impulse . . . to self-delight', a spontaneous reaching out for sensual pleasure which Tess shares with other animals — or would share if it were not for her sense of guilt, which Hardy sees as the imposition of society upon individuals who follow impulses which no shade of conscience forbids to other creatures. When Clare finally discovers the story of Tess's past life, he cannot see her as the woman he has fallen in love with. Her appeal for forgiveness falls on deaf ears:

> 'Forgive me as you are forgiven! *I* forgive *you*, Angel.'
> 'You — yes, you do.'
> 'But you do not forgive me?'
> 'O Tess, forgiveness does not apply to the case. You were one person; now you are another. My God — how can forgiveness meet such a grotesque — prestidigitation as that.'[19]

Clare's use of the word 'prestidigitation' suggests that he has been victim of a trick; by some act of conjuring Tess has changed from the maiden of his dreams to a tainted woman with an unforgivable past. What he says here echoes the premonition Tess had before the wedding. In Chapter Thirty-three, as she prepares to go to church with Angel Clare, Hardy repeats the imagery we have noticed already, which emphasises the veil of ignorance and misunderstanding that separates the couple, although they are not aware of it.

> In dressing, Tess moved about in a mental cloud of many coloured idealities, which eclipsed all sinister contingencies by its brightness,

and

Upheld by the momentum of time Tess ... did not see anything; did not know the road they were taking to the church. She knew that Angel was close to her; all the rest was a luminous mist. She was a sort of celestial person, who owed her being to poetry – one of those classical divinities Clare was accustomed to talk to her about when they took their walks together.[20]

But in heart of hearts Tess is capable of seeing herself clearly. As she kneels in prayer in her own room at Talbothays before they set off together for their honeymoon, we read:

'O my love, my love, why do I love you so?' she whispered there alone; 'for she you love is not my real self, but one in my image; the one I might have been.'[21]

We have looked in some detail at the structure of the central section of *Tess of the d'Urbervilles* because a close study of it reveals the very considerable difference between the reduced version of the novel, from which we began, and the complex issues which are revealed when account is taken of the nature of the narrative, the commentary of the narrator, the significance of the repeated patterns of imagery, not all of which operate in the same way or at the same level. This central strand of associated imagery – clouds, mist, dust, pollen – draws our attention to a fundamental theme in *Tess of the d'Urbervilles*, namely, the blindness of men and women to what lies outside their own purposes and desires. Human egotism – that impulse to see the rest of the world only as it affects oneself – distorts our capacity for seeing things as they are in themselves. This general truth about human beings – as Hardy sees them – is examined in detail in the working out of the relationship between Tess and Angel Clare.

The world of *Tess of the d'Urbervilles* is complex. In so far as it is non-human it is governed by chance and instinct: in so far as human beings are physical objects they are subject to chance; in so far as they are animal they are subject to irrational forces of impulse and animal pleasure. Capable as they are of thought, imagination and speech, they seem to be superior to the rest of the animal kingdom, but these special virtues are limited by the fact that they are subordinated to more primitive parts of our nature. Human rationality is subject to error: the systems of belief it creates are often at odds with the world as it really is. Hardy goes to some lengths to combat the view that the world is made for the satisfaction of men, that there is some pre-ordained harmony between its movements and the desires of the human heart. In nineteenth-century England one major way of reconciling men to the world in which they lived was through the tenets of Christianity. Hence, part of the novel deals with the narrowing effect upon Angel Clare and his family of beliefs which are rooted in the meagre soil of human speculation rather than in the truth.

Hardy's attitude to Christianity, however, is itself complex. Though Tess has many weaknesses which are specifically human, she has one overriding virtue which is not common among men and women, though exceptional people display it: it is the capacity for love. We do not mean by that word those pure and unreflective feelings of sexual attachment which seem to arise spontaneously and are evidence of a simple desire for the pleasurable extension of the life of the individual. Tess has those feelings, of course, and Hardy does justice to them. But the love which Tess has for Angel goes beyond them: her love survives his desertion of her and the hardships she suffers in his absence. Hardy's conception of love of this kind is drawn from Christian sources. When Tess exclaims to Clare, before their marriage, that she is not worthy of him, he says:

> 'I won't have you speak like it, dear Tess. Distinction does not consist in the facile use of a contemptible set of conventions but in being numbered among those who are true and honest, and just, and pure, and lovely, and of good report — as you are, my Tess.'[22]

The words Angel uses here are taken from St Paul's letter to the Philippians (Chapter 4, v. 8–9) and are an expression of a Christian assessment of what constitutes the good and admirable character. Elsewhere in the novel, and especially as Tess faces the difficulties of her life with uncomplaining endurance, Hardy applies to her other well-known words from the Bible. Just after Tess and Clare are married, we read:

> Clare knew that she loved him — every curve of her form showed that — but he did not know at that time the full depth of her devotion, its single-mindedness, its meekness; what long suffering it guaranteed, what honesty, what endurance, what good faith.[23]

No-one who reads these words can fail to be reminded of the description of Love (or Charity) in St Paul's First Epistle to the Corinthians, Chapter 13:

> Charity suffereth long and is kind; charity envieth not; charity vaunteth not itself, is not puffed up, doth not behave itself unseemly, seeketh not her own, is not easily provoked, thinketh no evil; rejoiceth not in iniquity but rejoiceth in the truth; beareth all things, believeth all things, hopeth all things, endureth all things.[24]

And Hardy himself makes the borrowing explicit when he says (in Chapter Thirty-six):

> Tess took everything as her deserts, and hardly opened her mouth. The firmness of her devotion to him [Clare] was indeed almost pitiful; quick-tempered as she naturally was, nothing that he could say made her unseemly; she sought not her own; was not provoked; thought no evil of his treatment of her. She might just now have been Apostolic Charity herself returned to a self-seeking modern world.[25]

She might, in other words, be an embodiment of the ideal description of Love which the Apostle Paul has given in his letter to the Corinthians.

Perhaps we may now attempt to sum up some of the aspects of the structure of *Tess of the d'Urbervilles* which we have discussed. The novel takes place within a certain period of time which helps to impose a rhythm on the events that are recorded. Its action consists of three main episodes which form a unified whole. It is set in (mainly) three places, which are so arranged as to follow the downward trajectory of Tess's life as it moves towards a tragic conclusion. The action of the novel is an example of a more general case which Hardy wishes to argue about the nature of human life: it is dominated by chance; its remarkable features, which distinguish it from the rest of the natural world, have severe limitations that often render it less successful than forms of life which are more simply constituted. By its nature human society is conventional: those exceptional individuals who break its conventions may suffer misunderstanding, or hostility. In the particular society which Hardy was concerned with, women suffered from special disadvantages, which might be increased if they belonged to a lowly social class. Christianity, which was the religion of the society Hardy wished to portray, had neglected the penetrating moral and spiritual insights of its founders, and had become narrowly rule-bound, censorious, class-bound, unforgiving.

Why, then, did Tess have to die? Some readers, relying on Hardy's famous sentence, 'The President of the Immortals had finished his sport with Tess', will say, as Tess's countrymen would no doubt have said, 'It had to be.' Fate pursued her, for malign purposes of its own. The answer given here is more complicated: human life is a chancy affair; human law takes little account of the circumstances of actions of which it disapproves (though it has to be said that English law today is more humane in this respect than in Hardy's time); to free herself from an intolerable sexual domination, Tess had committed murder; the failure of her marriage with Angel was partly her own fault, though most of the blame, perhaps, must rest on Angel's narrow human sympathy, warped as it was by a religious outlook which he mistakenly thought he had rejected.

Many of the details of the novel suggest that Tess's fate is likely to be unfortunate: think of the bad omens which occur throughout – the pointed shaft that pierces Prince, the horse, like a sword, and spills his blood in a pool on the road; the thorn of the rose that pricks Tess's chin; the d'Urberville coach; the evil omen of the Cross-in-Hand; the piece of blood-stained paper which flies in the wind near the gate of Clare's parents' house; the blow on the mouth which Tess delivers to Alec d'Urberville when he speaks slightingly of Clare. All these seem to lead – like clues in a paper-chase – to the scarlet stain, like the ace of hearts, which Alec's blood makes on his landlady's ceiling. But perhaps this sequence of imagery testifies to the consistency of Hardy's design, rather than to the inevitability of Tess's fate. Another pattern of imagery which supports and reflects the action of the novel centres on the sun. The central section of the novel is bathed in a sunlight that reflects the passionate love which develops between Tess and Angel Clare. But a close reading of the text will reveal that Hardy uses the sun imagery in a precise and detailed way to illustrate the fluctuating attitudes of Tess towards her feelings for Angel Clare.

The intention in this chapter has not been to explore every aspect of *Tess of the d'Urbervilles*. Perhaps enough has been said to suggest the richness of this novel; the reader may care to consider the topics which have been merely hinted at here. Hardy's novel is not easy to discuss because it contains many layers of meaning, not all of which are fully developed, but which represent ways of interpreting the novel that have their own validity. Hardy's novels speak with many voices: the test of a good reading of his novels is just how well the reader has been able to tolerate the apparent discordancies and contradictions: less successful readings force them into an over-simplified unanimity.

8 *The Novel in English: Some Forms of Modern Fiction*

Our study of *Tess of the d'Urbervilles* has perhaps suggested the complexity of design that might be found in the novels we read. The 'story' is a vehicle for many other narrative and linguistic devices which carry the larger meanings of the novel. Contrasted characters, complex patterns of imagery, subtle and extensive literary, religious and philosophical allusions, a use of language which has a poetic richness of implication are only some of the means that Hardy uses in the construction of his novel. Even so, Hardy stood on the brink of a period of self-conscious experimentation with the novel form which is associated with the names of Joseph Conrad (1857–1924), Ford Madox Ford (1873–1939), James Joyce (1882–1941), Virginia Woolf (1882–1941), William Faulkner (1897–1962), Malcolm Lowry (1909–57), Vladimir Nabokov (1899–1977) and many others. This period of ferment and inventiveness lasted from the end of the nineteenth century until about 1936. Since then there have been periods of reaction to more traditional forms and periods when novelty and experimentation were once again in fashion. It is roughly true that the history of the novel has always been divided between those who were excited by their subject-matter and those who were primarily concerned with the shaping of what they had to say. Needless to say, the constant preoccupation of the serious novelist is to find some form which most completely expresses the nature of the material he has before his mind.

If this book prepares the student to read Joyce's *A Portrait of the Artist as a Young Man* (1916), D. H. Lawrence's *Women in Love* (1920), E. M. Forster's *A Passage to India* (1924), Virginia Woolf's *To the Lighthouse* (1927) or William Faulkner's *The Sound and the Fury* (1929), its intention will have been fully realised. Such novels pose more difficult, but not essentially different, problems for the reader than those which have been tackled here. The student who has learned to look at the language and structure of the novel in the ways suggested here may approach more difficult texts with reasonable confidence. Our concern in this chapter is not with the experimental novel but rather with novels in English which were not written in one of the predominantly English-speaking countries of the world, or which were written in circumstances in which the language might develop in new and striking ways. One of the notable developments of the twentieth century has been the flowering of the novel in English worldwide. Is it possible to make some assessment of how such novels stand in relation to the tradition sketched here? What forms of the novel have the novelists of India, Africa or the Caribbean found for the distinctive material with which they have dealt? In other words, is the artistic grammar and vocabulary of the English novel universally available for use as is the language itself?

It is perhaps surprising how easily the methods and techniques developed during the history of the novel have been adapted to afford insight into the ways of life of rural India, modern Kenya or Nigeria. If this is indeed the case, two considerations might suggest themselves: perhaps changes in society throughout the world may have been brought about by similar forces. Industrialisation in Africa may have produced circumstances not unlike those Hardy saw taking place in England at the end of the nineteenth century. People packed together in cities, whether in Chicago or in Lagos, may offer broadly comparable material for the novelist. A second consideration is that the choice of English as a medium may predispose the writer to the concepts which have already been expressed in the language; writers of literature in English are likely to be influenced by the literary traditions of the language itself. To take some obvious, and perhaps trivial, examples, Chinua Achebe found an apt title for his first novel, *Things Fall Apart* (1958) in a line of the Irish poet, W. B. Yeats (1865–1939), who also wrote in the English tradition; Ngugi wa Thiong'o also found some organising principle for his novel, *Petals of Blood* (1977), in the same poem. But the African, Indian, West Indian, Australian or New Zealand writer must be conscious of many traditions, some written, some oral. In the end what distinguishes the talented novelist from the merely run-of-the-mill is how far he has found a voice and a technique of his own which will express a distinctive and memorable literary vision.

The relation of the non-English writer in English to the rich and varied traditions, literary and oral, indigenous and foreign, English, European and American, to which he is heir, is a fathomless study. The intention of this chapter is to look briefly at how some of these novelists have used the resources so far described. Have they remained within them, gone beyond them or turned their back on them in search of more appropriate techniques? We shall look in some detail at novels by R. K. Narayan, Chinua Achebe and Ngugi wa Thiong'o.

When we think of the novels of R. K. Narayan (1907–   ), perhaps we think mainly of a voice. Though he writes about India, he does so in a way which has obvious affinities with the classic novelists of nineteenth-century literature. As a student of English, he is thoroughly familiar with its literature, though there is nothing academic about his interest in it. An extract from *The English Teacher* (1945) may suggest the flavour of his novels. The protagonist, Krishna, is reading some letters he has received from his father and his wife, who is living in her father's house some distance from the school where Krishna teaches:

> My father's letter brought back to me not only the air of the village and all my childhood, but along with it all the facts – home, coconut-garden, harvest, revenue demand. He had devoted nearly a paragraph to my mother's health with a faint suggestion of complaint that she was not looking after herself quite properly – still keeping late hours for food – the last to eat in the house and still reluctant to swallow the medicines given to her. . . .
>
> And then came a paragraph of more immediate interest to me. 'Your father-in-law has written a letter today. I hear that by God's grace, your wife Susila, and the baby, are keeping well. He suggests that you should take her and the baby and set up a family and not live in a hostel any longer. He has my entire concurrence in this matter, as I think in the best interests of yourself you should set up a family. You have been in the hostel too long and I don't feel you ought to be wasting the best of your life in the hostel as it will affect your health and outlook. Your mother is also of the same view since your father-in-law's place is not a very healthy one for an infant. If you have no serious objection to this, your father-in-law suggests the 10th of next month as the most suitable and auspicious date . . .'
>
> He was a B.A. of the olden days brought up on Pater and Carlyle and Scott and Browning; personally looked after by Dr. William Miller, Mark Hunter and other eminent professors of Madras College; he was fastidious and precise in handling the English language, though with a very slight pomposity inevitable in the men of those days. After passing his B.A. he refused to enter government service,

as many of his generation did, but went back and settled in his village and looked after his land and property. I said to myself on reading his letter: 'God, what I am to do with a little child of seven months? . . .'[1]

The letter from Krishna's wife 'carried with it the fragrance of her trunk, in which she always kept her stationery – a mild jasmine smell surrounded her and all her possessions ever since he had known her'.[2]

What might strike the reader about Narayan's writing is its apparent willingness to tolerate irrelevance. There is a fluctuating waywardness about it: what have the details about Krishna's father's education to do with the announcement of his family's arrival in Malgudi? Of what importance is the smell of his wife's writing-paper? The novel carries the answers to these questions, so much so that the passage quoted above comes to seem the nucleus of the whole novel. The impermanence of life and of human relationships is the theme of Narayan's early work. After the death of Krishna's wife (when the redundancy and helpless charm of the early chapters give place to a strained, bare prose which conveys the dazed poignancy of bereavement), the child becomes the centre of his life. The conviction that his dead wife is communicating with him from beyond the grave coincides with Krishna's dissatisfaction with his work as an English teacher. He begins the process of shaking off his Western education to search for a deeper spiritual experience more in keeping with his own tradition. Though the point is not explicitly made in the novel, he is re-enacting the pattern of his father's life in returning to work with his own people. In the same way the jasmine scent from his wife's letter has its place in the structure of the novel. It becomes so powerfully associated with her that Krishna uses the name of the flower as his private name for her. In the final page of the novel, in which he is mystically reunited with her, as if she were still alive, it is with a garland of jasmine that he salutes her resurrected presence.

Looking back at the quotation from which we started, we can see that the design of Narayan's novel directs the reader's attention to what he thinks is of enduring value amidst the fluctuations and uncertainty of human experience. The concern of the novelist is with recording the process of self-development of the novel's protagonist. But there is nothing narrowly egotistic about this search for Krishna's true self: it is partly forced upon him by external circumstance. The arrival of his family, which he at first regards as a doubtful blessing, is the true beginning of his life. His love for his wife involves values and allegiances which are more than merely personal: they are not broken by her death. Some readers may find it difficult to accept Narayan's account of Krishna's spiritualistic encounters with his dead wife. But like Krishna's father, Narayan is 'fastidious and precise in handling the English language'. The narrative voice of the novel is not lightly to be disbelieved.

What then is Narayan's novel? Is it a realistic account of how a young Hindu rejected the rationalism of his English education to return to concepts which sit uneasily with it? Is it a record of a move from 'common sense' to other-worldliness, which might alienate readers not in sympathy with a belief in life after death? Surely there is some inescapable truth in these suggestions. But it would be wrong to read the novel in a wholly literal way. Narayan never loses touch with the inconsistencies of experience: the hard facts of life's contingency save him from idealism and tragedy. And the contingencies of Narayan's world are usually absurd: cheerfulness keeps breaking through. Nevertheless, Narayan finds, this world of comically hard facts must allow a place for the spirit. That is what endures in a world of illusion: his dead wife represents – indeed, is – that spiritual world. Turning towards her, he becomes more truly himself. So she becomes his spiritual guide, and he turns away from his books to his own child, and then to the care and education of other children. (Another humble Indian schoolteacher, whose family is a hindrance to him, serves as a parallel figure to Krishna in the novel: rejecting his family, he becomes a holy man to devote himself to his teaching.) Now the reader may remember that Krishna's wife has always been slightly at odds with his European interests: though she shares his interest in reading, somehow her plans to develop her education never come off. When he reads poetry to her, she finds in the poems perfectly justifiable occasions for wildly mocking laughter. The direction she points Krishna towards in death is not different from what she signalled in life: it is simply more authoritative. So Susila – and jasmine – become symbols for the Indian consciousness which Krishna was in danger of losing.

Narayan's previous novel, *The Bachelor of Arts* (1937), may appear to have an even more random surface structure. It recounts the experiences of Chadran as he gains his B.A., wonders what to do with his life, falls unsuccessfully in love, abandons his identity for a brief experience as a holy man, returns home to become an agent for a newspaper, and by the end of the novel is uncertainly launched on a marriage arranged for him by his family. Readers of *The Bachelor of Arts* may run the risk of thinking it a charming series of humorous sketches of Indian provincial life. But its theme is randomness: Chandra's life is ruled by chance; the short-term goals of academic success, or of success in love, bring no satisfaction. Narayan surely wished his readers to draw their own conclusions about the unsatisfactoriness of Chandra's life of illusion; he offers his sketch of it without comment, but *The English Teacher* is perhaps the best comment on *The Bachelor of Arts*.

In *The Guide* (1958) Narayan dovetails two narratives with great skill: one, in the present, is the story of how Raju, the convict, was taken for a saint by some simple villagers; the other is the story of how he moved from being a shopkeeper to being a guide to being the manager of a 'star' dancer. They coincide at the point when the villagers believe that Raju is prepared to fast to death to bring them rain, and Raju confesses what he really is to the man who first consulted him as a spiritual guide. But Raju's confession has no effect: he is still a saint in the villager's eyes and the fast to the death goes on. The structure of *The Guide* is essential to its effectiveness: the parallel narratives of Raju's lives generate the ironies of the novel. Raju the convict cancels Raju the saint, but Raju the saint cancels Raju the convict. Neither story is self-evidently more authentic than the other. In contrast to *The English Teacher*, there is no simple opposition between illusion and reality. There seems to be no end to the layers of illusion in Raju's life, unless Narayan means to suggest to us that even a pretence of holiness may mysteriously lead to the real thing.

Despite what has been said about *The English Teacher*, symbolism is a less significant feature of Narayan's novels than is his management of the action. The setting of Malgudi is developed in the most interesting and attractive way, but it is surely the qualities of intelligence and humour in the narrative voice of these novels which give them their strong appeal.

Narayan's approach to novel writing seems nearer to Jane Austen than to Thomas Hardy or to most contemporary novelists: how is he to be compared with a younger generation of novelists? Chinua Achebe, twenty years younger than Narayan, published *Things Fall Apart* in 1958. This novel is quite different in character from those of Narayan. Although it is written in English, it deals with a way of life which, initially at least, has not been touched by European influence: it is, of course, the point of the novel to describe the effect of foreign attitudes and beliefs on the complex, unified system of Ibo village life sometime in the 1890s. *Things Fall Apart* has some of the characteristics of history: it recounts the life of Okonkwo, a powerful man, who represents qualities of simple manliness on which he prides himself. The novel is steeped in the folk-lore of the Ibo; its characters speak easily in proverbs and with reference to traditional fables transmitted through generations. Life in the system of villages which constitutes Umuofia is regulated by custom and ceremony; the worlds of the living and the dead are near neighbours. People move naturally, but yet mysteriously, from their everyday social roles to their other-worldly functions as priestess or representative of the ancestral spirits of the village, where their powers are wide, their authority absolute, their appearance strange and terrifying.

The language of *Things Fall Apart* – the narrative voice of the novel – can be seen as an extension of the traditional wisdom of the proverbs and fables of the tribe. Achebe has found a style which matches his traditional material. It is impersonal, plain, undramatic but deeply impressive. Consider the following passage; after seven years of exile, Okonkwo has returned to his native village:

Seven years was a long time to be away from one's clan. A man's place was not always there, waiting for him. As soon as he left, someone else rose and filled it. The clan was like a lizard; if it lost its tail it soon grew another.

Okonkwo knew these things. He knew that he had lost his place among the nine masked spirits who administered justice in the clan. He had lost the chance to lead his war-like clan against the new religion, which, he was told, had gained ground. He had lost the years in which he might have taken the highest titles in the clan. But some of these losses were not irreparable. He was determined that his return should be marked by his people. He would return with a flourish, and regain the seven wasted years.

Even in his first year of exile he had begun to plan for his return. The first thing he would do would be to rebuild his compound on a more magnificent scale. He would build a bigger barn than he had had before and he would build huts for two new wives. Then he would show his wealth by initiating his sons with the *ozo* society. Only the really great men in the clan were able to do this. Okonkwo saw clearly the high esteem in which he would be held, and he saw himself taking the highest title in the land.[3]

The style of *Things Fall Apart* seems to express the soul of the people it deals with. It understands and accepts their assumptions and modes of thought. When it describes Okonkwo, it enters into his plans and expectations, without setting any distance between Okonkwo and the voice which tells his story. The syntax of Achebe's sentences is not complicated. Okonkwo's thoughts are described directly, without qualification or elaboration: he is a direct, uncomplicated man. These sentences seem to mirror Okonkwo's thought-processes, as they move from idea to idea, clearly and deliberately. Their repetitions ('He had lost his place . . . he had lost the chance . . . he had lost the years.') suggest the slow brooding of his mind as he remembers and reflects and plans for the future. Looking from the outside, the reader may judge Okonkwo to be a deeply selfish man, though his self-obsession is masked by his devotion to warrior ideals.

The narrator makes no such judgement, but the action of *Things Fall Apart* appears to carry its own critique of Okonkwo's values. Many of the episodes of the novel appear to have been selected to throw light on the opposed values which are attached to the concepts of 'male' and 'female' in Okonkwo's society. In Okonkwo's mind there is no doubt about the superiority of masculinity. To be weak is to be effeminate. So his father, a man who has taken no titles, had been a weakling, a womanish man. Nwoye, his son, who becomes converted to Christianity, is equally effeminate in his father's eyes. Yet many details point in another direction. When Okonkwo is exiled to his mother's village, he is reminded of the special value which is attached to the idea of motherhood; his daughter, Ezinma, who has qualities which would not disgrace a man, is particularly beloved by her father. When an old man of a neighbouring village dies, and his wife dies of grief, Obiereka, whose peaceful ways contrast with Okonkwo's belligerence, says:

> 'It was always said that Ndulue and Ozoemena had one mind . . . I remember when I was a young boy there was a song about them. He could not do anything without telling her.'
> 'I did not know that,' said Okonkwo. 'I thought he was a strong man in his youth.'
> 'He was indeed' . . .
> Okonkwo shook his head doubtfully.[4]

Okonkwo's values are differentiated from those of other elders of the clan, especially over the death of Ikemefuma, the hostage whom he kills on the orders of the Oracle of the Hills and Caves. Yet it is when the priestess of this Oracle carries off his daughter, Ezinma, that Okonkwo shows himself most of one mind with his wife, Ekwefi.

The art of Achebe is one of understatement. *Things Fall Apart* has the appearance of the most cunningly constructed boat, made of the simplest material, which is navigable over deep and unfathomable waters. Okonkwo is a man of great power, who is never less than impressive, yet of considerable inconsistency. In this he is perhaps a true representative of his clan. Achebe locates and exhibits the strengths as well as the shortcomings of the social system he describes, but it is for the reader to speculate on the degree of instability which the conflict of male and female values produces in Umuofia. The design of the novel does not allow any overt authorial comment on the matter. If Achebe intended the selection of the events of his narrative to carry a critique of the values of Okonkwo, and of Umuofia, the intention is left implicit. The reader does not forget the grief of the mother whose twins have been taken away to die; Nwoye does not forget the murder of his friend Ikumefema, nor is Okonkwo unaffected by what he had done, though he refuses to think of his feelings as other than unaccustomed 'womanliness'.

Nwoye, the mother of the twins and the outcasts of the village turn to the Christian missionaries who come to the area. But it is part of the tragedy of the situation that the white men are unable to understand the strengths of the clan. In the final section of the novel, Achebe is more concerned with the external threat to the clan's survival than with its internal inconsistencies. The events of the third section of the novel, which describes the violence between Umuofia and the white man, may lend support to Okonkwo's belief that aggressiveness is an indispensable attribute of masculinity. Nwoye, the gentle son and Christian convert, has no part to play here. Obiereka now appears as Okonkwo's apologist, when he says of him to the District Officer:

'That man was one of the greatest men in Umuofia. You drove him to kill himself; and now he will be buried like a dog. . . .'[5]

And it is Obiereka who expresses the corruption which the white man has brought to the people by setting members of the clan against one another:

'. . . The white man is very clever. He came quietly and peaceably with his religion. We were amused at his foolishness and allowed him to stay. Now he has won our brothers, and our clan can no longer act like one. He has put a knife on the things that held us together and we have fallen apart.'[6]

Readers may perhaps wonder whether in the situation Achebe has described, Christianity was not so much a knife as a catalyst, but that is not the metaphor Achebe has used. His technique of objective, third-person narration has allowed him to include a wide range of incidents whose implications do not always point one way. If the reader agrees with Obiereka's judgement on the cause of Okonkwo's death, what is he to think of those who did not adopt his violent solution to the problems of the clan? And what is to be made of the earlier critique of his warrior values? If his death is tragic, by what concept of tragedy is it judged to be so?

Things Fall Apart might usefully be compared with *The Mayor of Casterbridge* (1896), since Okonkwo's circumstances and fate have something in common with Michael Henchard, the protagonist of Hardy's novel. An interesting contrast, however, might be found in *A Grain of Wheat* by Ngugi wa Thiong'o where violence in defence of national independence is seen in a twentieth-century context. In contrast to Achebe's deceptive simplicity, this novel has a dense and complex narrative structure. Though its action takes place over five days of the week in which Kenya gained its independence, by entering into the memories of his characters, and by means of three long accounts of personal experience by leading figures in the novel, Ngugi surveys in detail some ten years of the history of Kenya's state of emergency and alludes to significant episodes in its political history stretching back to the days of Queen Victoria. But Ngugi's aim is not merely historical; of the two significant martyr figures in the novel, one, Kihima, the freedom-fighter, dies for liberty at the hands of the British; the other, Mugo, his betrayer, dies, we are left to assume, at the hands of his own people in the cause of truth.

But how necessary, and how successful, is the complexity of the narrative technique of Ngugi's novel? He uses a method by which events, which have occurred over a wide span of history, are embedded in the story of a week. It is as if a simple sentence such as, 'These things happened then', were so extended by dependent clauses that it becomes almost impossible to disentangle the substance of the main clause. What Ngugi gains by his maze of overlapping narratives is to show how closely connected are the lives of characters apparently widely separated by race, class, background and habits of mind. In constructing a fiction based on the real events of history, he has used narrative methods not unlike those Conrad used in creating the fictitious history of Costaguana in *Nostromo* (1904). What problems are created for the reader by such displacements of chronology, and what benefits do they bring to the achievement of the purposes of the novel?

The examples given above might suggest some of the ways in which writers of the novel in English have adapted established techniques in the search for a form appropriate to the new material they have sought to express. Powerful and ambitious attempts to find new forms may be seen in Ayi Kwei Armah's *Why are we so blest?* (1972) and *Two Thousand Seasons* (1977) in which language is used in a poetic and visionary way which has affinities with William Faulkner and the French *nouveau roman*. Caribbean writers such as George Lamming (1927–   ) and Wilson Harris (1921–   ) also write in non-naturalistic forms where vision, dream and fable are the substance of novels whose language is poetic, surreal, and perhaps more purely imaginative than that of the novelists who have been considered so far.

9 *Conclusion: Some Basic Concepts Reviewed*

To conclude this introduction to the novel it is worth reviewing some of the general concepts which have been discussed in previous chapters, and which have been used to illuminate our consideration of individual novels. Is it possible to generalise about works of art which are so diverse, complex and unpredictable? Perhaps the only rule about novel-writing is that there are no rules. Novelists work within a tradition of writing which has a history but no laws. Writers will be influenced by their own experience, their own conception of the form of the novel, and by the 'languages' which they have at their command. Experience will have made them feel at home with certain areas of life, with certain ways of behaving and talking, with certain themes, recurrent situations or images which seem to haunt their imagination. As we read through the work of most novelists, we begin to detect characteristic ways of working: there are detectable 'family resemblances' between them which make them characteristically Dickensian, or enable us to talk about 'the world of Iris Murdoch'. We shall look at some of the most general technical terms which are in use in talking about fiction, simply to remind the student of features worth identifying and thinking about in any novel which he or she may be required to read.

Plot

This is the most general term used to describe the design of a novel. Very often it is restricted to mean 'a summary of the principal events of the novel'. But this is too narrow an approach: in our use of the word, 'plot' means the complete pattern or design of the work. It is composed of all the elements which, taken together, suggest the direction, or tendency of the work. It is the way in which the author has arranged his material so that it can be seen as having an analysable form, or meaning. This form need not be simple: the events of one day, 16 June 1904, comprise the material of James Joyce's *Ulysses*. The novel is based on a scheme drawn from the *Odyssey* of the ancient Greek epic poet, Homer: but Joyce's scheme demands a virtuosic display of different varieties of language and involves a very large number of characters with their own aims and purposes. It is far from easy to see what deeper principles are implied by the extraordinarily varied sections of the book. Despite the existence of a number of clearly marked 'themes' – the relation of father to son, of husband to wife, the relationships of the variety of contemporary modes of living and thinking to one another, the relationship of the present to the past, or of life on this earth to the rest of the universe – it would be extremely difficult to say what the book (can it be called a novel at all?) is about. Contrary to the view that *Ulysses* is a unique work which has produced no successors, many modern novels have been written as long, densely written, mysterious texts, so full of surface detail of a strange and puzzling kind that they may almost be regarded as magical books, works which are designed to challenge, and perhaps defeat, the reader's powers of interpretation. They invite comparison with religious texts; they aim to be repositories of esoteric wisdom, which do not 'tell' the reader anything, but which initiate him into techniques of meditation by showing him the extraordinary 'alternative worlds' which can be made with words. Writers such as Vladimir Nabokov, Thomas Pynchon (1937–   ), William Gaddis (1922–   ) and John Fowles (1926–   ) may be thought to belong to this category.

The novels of such writers almost defy the concept of plot because the term itself suggests 'closure'; it implies that it will have an intelligible structure which will yield itself up to analysis. It is with novels of this kind which we have been principally concerned. Novels of the eighteenth and nineteenth centuries have a discernible structure which is often carried explicitly in the novel itself. It is only towards the end of the nineteenth century that the novelist withdraws, leaving the structure of the novel to express its own nature. But what if there were a very large number of designs which a given number of words or chapters might express? What if the structure of the novel were designed to express randomness?

Some modern writers have been fascinated by the idea of 'multiple meanings', by the thought that interpretation is an endless process, to which the writer should not set bounds. Books of this kind make very great demands on the interpretative skill of readers. Whereas formerly novelists accepted the responsibility of making clear the boundaries of meaning, now that task (or, as some might put it, pleasure) has been left to the reader.

The notion of plot, then, covers the principles (explicit or implicit) which govern the development and arrangement of the material out of which the novel has been made. These will include action and characters, that is, what people do and why they do it; the commentary of the narrator, whether the narrator is a separate character in the novel or whether he is the explicit or implicit voice of the author himself; the symbolic scheme of the novel, if there is any; the verbal patterns, or repeated patterns of imagery, by which the words and actions of the characters are supported, illustrated or interpreted.

Realism and Fantasy

A historically important division of the novel may be made between those which aim to offer an impression of factual and historical accuracy and those which do not. In an earlier chapter we quoted the opinion of the American novelist, Nathaniel Hawthorne, on what was the essential feature of the novel. But he distinguished another kind of writing, which he called the 'romance', and which in modern times has become almost more characteristic of the novel as a form than the 'realistic' novel itself. Hawthorne wanted to distinguish between works of fiction which professed to give an account of the ordinary and works of fiction which included the extraordinary, or the marvellous. Here is a fuller quotation from his preface to *The House of the Seven Gables* (1851):

> When a writer calls his work a Romance, it need hardly be observed that he wishes to claim a certain latitude, both as to its fashion and material, which he would not have felt himself entitled to assume had he professed to be writing a Novel. The latter form of composition is presumed to aim at very minute fidelity, not merely to the possible, but to the probable and ordinary course of man's experience. The former – while, as a work of art, it must rigidly subject itself to laws, and while it sins unpardonably so far as it may swerve aside from the truth of the human heart – has fairly a right to present that truth under circumstances, to a great extent, of the writer's choosing or creation. If he thinks fit, also he may so manage

his atmospherical medium as to bring out or mellow the lights and deepen and enrich the shadows of the picture. He will be wise, no doubt, to make a very moderate use of the privileges here stated, and, especially, to mingle the Marvellous rather as a slight, delicate, and evanescent flavour, than as any portion of the actual substance of the dish offered to the public. He can hardly be said, however, to commit a literary crime even if he disregarded this caution.[1]

Twentieth-century novelists have been very much more aware of how short a distance lies between the ordinary and the marvellous. A dedication to being truthful about 'the truth of the human heart' has extended the range of subject-matter which novelists feel free to discuss and has increased the freedom with which they present it. The Russian novelist, Bulgakov (1891–1940), for example, wrote an extraordinary novel – *The Master and Margarita* (published posthumously in 1966–7) – which combined an account of what might have happened if the Devil had visited Moscow in the nineteen-thirties with a quasi-historical account of the trial and execution of Jesus of Nazareth. In *Lord of the Flies* (1954), William Golding (1911–   ) has written a brilliant and chastening novel on what might have happened if a group of boys had been marooned on a desert island. A growing awareness of the extraordinary nature of the world of fact as well as the internal world of fantasy has made what Hawthorne called the Romance very much more the standard type of the novel than the depiction of the possible and the probable which he called the novel. Novels, then, are works of the imagination; they carry with them the impression of the writer's cast of mind. To talk of the design of a novel is to talk about how the writer sees the world. Every element of the structure of a novel – from plot to sentence – shows us something of the character of the author. The book is a way of seeing things which has been put into words. Perhaps it would be better to say, 'It is a way of *saying* things', a way of grasping the world in words. The design of a novel presents the nature of the world as it is refracted through the unique structure of one writer's mind, just as light refracted through a crystal throws a characteristic image on a screen.

Narrative

Novels are narrated – they are told to the reader by one of the characters, by an independent narrator (sometimes, the author himself, or the version of himself which he cares to present to the public) or they are reported to the reader in an apparently impersonal way. Not everything in a novel can be narrated at the same pace: now the narrator will linger, now he will hurry on. Some of the material will be narrated in summary form; some in close detail. Now we shall be told what is happening, now (apparently) we shall be *shown*. We shall hear what the characters said and did; sometimes we shall be allowed to share their thoughts and feelings.

The presentation of a novel depends upon *the point of view* from which it is told. This term somewhat resembles the notion of perspective in painting. It suggests that there is one spot from which the picture, or the action of the novel, is best seen. It suggests ideas of depth and distance: some parts of the canvas will appear nearer the spectator than others. It suggests, too, that the spectator's eyes are not completely free: the picture has an internal logic; the observer's eye is guided by the structure of what he observes.

When the student considers the 'point of view' of the novel he should ask himself the following questions: is there a narrator who appears to know everything about what happens in the novel, including the thoughts, feelings and intentions of the characters? Or, if there is, is there a limit to his knowledge? Consider, for example, Conrad's *Lord Jim*: we know everything about what happened, but about the thoughts and intentions of the principal agent in the novel we can only speculate. There may be no independent narrator at all; the story may be told directly in the first person by one of the characters, or indirectly in the third person using only the knowledge that one of the characters might be reasonably supposed to have. Henry James's novel *The Ambassadors* selects one of the characters and presents him so that the whole of the action is seen through his eyes and the eyes of a lady whom he makes friends with. But while we are allowed access to the thoughts and feelings of the principal character, Lambert Strether, we are only allowed to hear what his friend, Maria Gostrey, has to say to him – and so on for the other characters in the novel.

Some modern novelists have been so determined that their readers will be solely responsible for understanding what happens in their novels that they withhold all commentary and explanation, offering a quite impersonal account of what the characters do and say. The extreme example of this kind is the novel which is as far as possible conducted in dialogue. Here, the distinction between the novel and the play is almost obliterated. When you are studying a novel, think about the relative weight which is given to what you are told, and what you are shown. Consider, too, whether there is any discrepancy between them which might suggest that neither action nor commentary is to be trusted. Is there any irony in the tone of the narrative which suggests we should not take the characters at face value? How much has the novelist relied on the reader to complete a line of interpretation which may be hinted at but not made explicit? Are the conversations between the characters explicitly commented upon by the narrator? If not, what is their function in the novel? Does the writer tell us unequivocally what we are to believe about his novel (and, if so, do we believe him?) or is there an essential role for the reader in making inferences or coming to judgements, without which the novel will be incomplete? Is the novelist asking us to follow him, or to find out for ourselves?

Action

In the preceding chapters the word 'action' has been used to refer to a restricted part of the design of the novel; it refers to what the characters in the novel do, and it is taken for granted that in most novels what takes place will be human action. (In some novels animals or mythical creatures may be the main characters, but even in those the motivation of the action is conceived in human terms.) Human action is assumed to be free, purposeful, collaborative and foresightful. Human agents are moved by many causes, emotional and rational. Their aims and purposes are pursued with varying degrees of understanding of consequences and sense of responsibility. Over the last century or so, however, it has become accepted that human action is not always self-aware and conscious of its own purposes. The novel, however, has been a store-house of case histories which threw light on the psychology of human behaviour long before its formalisation in theoretical terms. Jane Austen's *Emma*, for example, is just such an examination of the unconscious side of human personality. Jane Austen is a master analyst of the unacknowledged assumptions which are revealed in the speech habits of families or individuals, the self-deception which covers the aggressive and hostile aspects of human interaction.

   Novelists differ in their treatment of human action; for some, it is the excitement of the event which matters; for others, it is the pursuit of the minute links in the chain of motives which lead to action, or the careful analysis of the consequences of choice. Of all English novelists in the nineteenth century George Eliot has the strongest sense of the moral seriousness of the act of choice. In a famous simile she sees history as a kind of Nemesis, watching the inevitable consequences of her characters' actions working themselves out through unforeseen ramifications. Studies of this kind do not end with individuals: people are strongly influenced by the society in which they have grown up. The complicated network made out of the consequences of individual decisions becomes a map of the moral attitudes of a society.

Action in the novel need not be of this kind. If the author wishes to puzzle or intrigue or entertain, the reader may be willing to accept behaviour that is unlikely, unconventional or absurd because it is enjoyable to do so. The conventions of comedy or farce make concern with the consequences of behaviour irrelevant; detective novels are rarely interested in the consequences of crime. On the other hand, what people do in novels may be subordinated to some larger pattern of ideas; behaviour may be seen as typical or representative, and so its individual characteristics are less significant than its capacity for suggesting the average or normal. If the author wishes to advocate ideas which he believes in, the pattern of the action may be contrived to conform with these ideas. How much of an individual is Jack, or Ralph, or Piggy in *Lord of the Flies* by William Golding; how much are they representative of character-types which society values to a greater or lesser degree? Novels of this kind may be stimulating tracts for the times (like *Animal Farm* (1946) by George Orwell), or they may be boring propaganda, mere vehicles for a point of view. But any novel will suffer if it fails to suggest that the characters it deals with are capable of independent action — unpredictability, perhaps, being a sign of what is truly human. Hence, too less careful patterning may suggest that the author is stamping his intentions too rigidly on his characters who need to have the degree of freedom (however small it may sometimes appear) which human beings assume they have for themselves.

Character

Character, action, and point of view are obviously closely linked. All of them are subordinate to the novel's overall design but in some novels a sense of pattern may be conveyed mainly through the action and the interplay of the characters. How is it that we can be persuaded of the existence of imaginary people who live only in the words of the novelist? Characters, after all, are constructs which we make out of their reported actions, the words they are given to say and the commentary made on them by their creator. Something must depend on how they are presented. Here, for example, is the first description of Mr Bounderby in *Hard Times* (1854) by Charles Dickens:

> He was a rich man: banker, merchant, manufacturer and what not. A big, loud man, with a stare and a metallic laugh. A man made out of coarse material, which seemed to have been stretched to make so much of him. A man with a great puffed head and forehead, swelled veins in his temples, and such a strained skin to his face that it seemed to hold his eyes open, and lift his eyebrows up. A man with a pervading appearance on him of being inflated like a balloon and ready to start. A man who could never sufficiently vaunt himself a self-made man. A man who was always proclaiming, through that brassy speaking-trumpet voice of his, his old ignorance and his old poverty. A man who was the Bully of humility.[2]

The picture we are given of Mr Bounderby combines mimicry with judgement. This succession of sentences, verbless, apart from the first, has something of the brusque, self-assertion of Mr Bounderby himself. Each sentence is no more than a noun with an adjective phrase or clause attached. And the noun is 'man'. What kind of man is Mr Bounderby, and how is the author's judgement conveyed to the reader? First, he is described in terms of his impressive occupations (but notice how dismissive that 'and what not' is of them). Clearly Dickens does not approve of Mr Bounderby: a man may forgivably be 'big', but not 'loud'; staring is not socially acceptable in English society, since it implies an invasion of the privacy of the object of the stare; 'metallic' laughs are harsh, jarring, unpleasant to listen to, and lacking in human warmth; Mr Bounderby does not consider the feelings of others; he is much too concerned to express himself. The next sentence carries a more subtle social judgement: Mr Bounderby is made of 'coarse material'; he is not refined, not a member of the decent middle classes; he has reached his present position from a much inferior one but his upward social progress has not altered his nature; 'stretch' suggests the distance he has travelled, and the strain of it, as well as the physical grossness which affluence has brought with it. If there is a touch of snobbery on the author's part here – a suggestion of 'Once a peasant, always a peasant' – Dickens expects his reader to share his view. The next sentences seize on this feature of Mr Bounderby: 'stretched' suggests 'puffed', 'swelled', 'strained', 'inflated'. 'Puffed', 'swelled' and 'inflated', in particular, have unflattering associations with self-advertisement and vanity. But another association of the word 'puffed' sets Mr Bounderby in a different frame of reference. Dickens describes him as exactly the opposite of St Paul's picture of the loving person (the description of Charity which Hardy used in his presentation of Tess): he *is* puffed up; he vaunteth himself; his voice is like a 'brassy speaking-trumpet'. And what it proclaims is his 'old ignorance and his old poverty'. In Mr Bounderby's mouth the word 'old' must mean 'former'; in the mouth of the author it is likely to suggest 'long-standing', 'ineradicable'. His ignorance and poverty are spiritual rather than material. Equally, there is just a hint of a play on words in 'Bully', which can mean 'the bosom friend' as well as 'the tyrant'. In other words, Mr Bounderby is a close friend of humility because he was born poor, but now he uses his previous background to exult over those who have failed to fight their way up the social ladder.

Making a character is a complex process involving work which must be done by author, character and reader. The author creates the character, but he presents him with many hints about how he is to be taken. If he does not do so overtly, the reader must be all the more vigilant to look for clues which will suggest how the character is to be understood. Sometimes an author may spring a surprise on the reader. Here is how a younger contemporary of Dickens, Wilkie Collins (1824–89) introduces one of his characters in *The Woman in White* (1860):

My first glance round me . . . disclosed a well-furnished breakfast-table, standing in the middle of a long room, with many windows in it. I looked from the table to the window farthest from me, and saw a lady standing at it with her back turned towards me. The instant my eyes rested on her, I was struck by the rare beauty of her form, and by the unaffected grace of her attitude. Her figure was tall, yet not too tall; comely and well-developed yet not fat; her head set on her shoulders with an easy, pliant firmness; her waist, perfection in the eyes of a man, for it occupied its natural place, it filled out its natural circle, it was visibly and delightfully undeformed by stays. She had not heard my entrance into the room; and I allowed myself the luxury of admiring her for a few moments, before I moved one of the chairs near me, as the least embarrassing means of attracting her attention. She turned towards me immediately. The easy elegance of every movement of her limbs and body as soon as she began to advance from the far end of the room, set me in flutter of expectation to see her face clearly. She left the window – and I said to myself, the lady is dark. She moved forwards a few steps – and I said to myself, the lady is young. She approached nearer – and I said to myself (with a sense of surprise which words failed me to express), the lady is ugly.[3]

Notice how repetitions of syntactical patterns set up expectations in the reader. The repetition of 'and I said to myself, the lady . . .' establishes a rhythm, an expectation of a pleasant experience, which is, first of all, held up by the long interruption before the final appearance of the phrase, after which the expectation is disappointed. Here we have a first-person narrator introducing a character to us: in fact the description tells us more about the narrator than about the character. Behind the narrator, of course, stands the author who has prepared this surprise for us. How much does this presentation tell us about the author? Certainly, the narrator enjoys looking at attractive women. He is pleased to have the chance to indulge his taste while the lady is looking out of the window. He is a practised and fastidious judge; his words of approval suggest the care with which he appraises her, and his skill in knowing 'the good points' of a woman: one might sense that he would take just as much care in judging a horse or a dog. At the same time, his terms of approval ('unaffected grace', 'easy, pliant firm-ness') might seem rather schoolboyish. Feminists might complain that there is something objectionable in presenting a female character as seen through 'the eyes of a man'. There is no sense of irony in the passage: the author seems sure that his reader will enjoy the description (and share the disappointment of its conclusion) just as much as the narrator. A critical reader might wonder why the author has chosen to present his character in this way: what tastes and interests does he imply in the reader whom he is addressing?

Characters are seen from a point of view: the one presented in the last example is a good illustration. It could be compared with a care-fully composed Victorian picture. A man in the foreground looks across a table at a woman lit by the light coming in through one of the windows of the room. (We may use our imagination to furnish the breakfast-table as we wish.) The physical description given of the woman is perfectly conventional – once again the reader is invited to fill out the minimal description Collins gives us. Indeed, when Collins presents a second female figure (one who is really attractive this time) he allows the narrator to say quite frankly to the reader:

> Think of her as you thought of the first woman who quickened the pulses within you that the rest of the sex had no art to stir. Let the kind, candid blue eyes meet yours as they met mine, with the one matchless look which we both remember so well. Let her voice speak the music that you once loved best, attuned as sweetly to your ear as to mine. Let her footsteps, as she comes and goes, in these pages, be like that other footstep to whose airy fall your own heart once beat time. Take her as the visionary nursling of your own fancy; and she will grow upon you, all the more clearly, as the living woman who lives in mine.[4]

Perhaps only writers of a lesser skill are quite so dependent upon the fantasies of their readers.

Characters in novels do not usually exist singly: they form part of a patterned group of people who are nothing if they do not speak and act. The pattern is sometimes a simple one of contrast: we become familiar with George Eliot's awkward, dark heroines who are usually contrasted with pretty, fair-haired, blue-eyed girls, who are attractive to men but of little interest otherwise. Alec d'Urberville and Angel Clare belong to opposite ends of a spectrum of masculinity, though other aspects of their personalities complicate any simple account of the differences between them. Readers of *Jane Eyre* (1847) will recall a much more straightforward contrast of masculine types in Mr Rochester and St John Rivers, the weak-spirited altruist, who wishes to use Jane for the good of others. One of the most impressive aspects of Dickens's genius is his ability to organise squadrons of characters within a coherent design. Equally memorable is his ability to create a character who lives forever in one or two phrases.

Here in *Our Mutual Friend* (1865) a nameless dinner-guest of the Veneerings, who are jumped-up *nouveaux riches* from nowhere, attempts to interpose between Mr Podsnap, the English patriot, and a gentleman from France:

> A youngish sallowish gentleman in spectacles, with a lumpy fore-head, seated in a supplementary chair at a corner of the table, here caused a profound sensation by saying, in a raised voice, 'ESKER',

and then stopping dead.

'Mais oui', said the foreign gentleman, turning towards him. 'Est-ce que? Quoi donc?'

But the gentleman with the lumpy forehead having for the time delivered himself of all that he found behind his lumps, spake for the time no more.

'I was enquiring,' said Mr Podsnap, resuming the thread of his discourse, 'Whether You Have Observed in our Streets as We should say, Upon our Pavvy as you would say, any Tokens —'

The foreign gentleman, with patient courtesy entreated pardon; 'But what was tokenz?'

'Marks', said Mr Podsnap; 'Signs, you know, Appearances — Traces!'

'Ah! Of a Orse?' enquired the foreign gentleman.

'We call it Horse', said Mr Podsnap, with forbearance. 'In England, Angleterre, England, We aspirate the "H" and we say "Horse". Only our Lower Classes Say "Orse"!'

'Pardon', said the foreign gentleman; 'I am alwiz wrong!'

'Our Language', said Mr Podsnap, with a gracious consciousness of being always right, 'is Difficult. Ours is a Copious Language, and Trying to Strangers. I will not Pursue my Question.'

But the lumpy gentleman, unwilling to give it up, again madly said 'ESKER', and again spake no more.[5]

Only in the amplest of novels would there be room for the gentleman who said 'ESKER', but even he has a perfectly understandable part to play in the design of the whole. Those last novels of Dickens were biting commentaries upon the state of the English nation. Mr Podsnap represents England in all its insularity and over-weening self-esteem. His condescending questions to the foreign gentleman imply that non-English speakers are fools: but the young man with the lumpy forehead (the lumps are supposed to indicate brains) demonstrates how foolish Englishmen are when they try to speak in a language other than their own. This vivid sketch of the tongue-tied Englishman helps to emphasise Mr Podsnap's own foolishness, even if that were not sufficiently demonstrated by the language he uses himself to the unfortunate Frenchman. But the reader treasures it for its own sake, for its brevity, its sharpness, its sense of fun — perhaps for its reminder of incidents when people have made fools of themselves, or when we have done so ourselves.

But how does Dickens make his effect? The -ishes of 'youngish' and 'sallowish' suggest mediocrity; the spectacles suggest earnestness; the lumpy forehead suggests pretensions to brains; the supplementary chair suggests that he is accidental, irrelevant, superfluous, unforeseen. The phrase 'having for the time being delivered himself of all that he found behind his lumps' suggests how far his brainy appearance is belied by the insubstantial mental vigour his words reveal. We sense the goodwill behind his attempt to translate Mr Podsnap's questions into French, but also the inadequacy of his effort, the growing panic as he finds how far he has fallen short of success. Even this nameless little figure (who never appears again) has a life and purpose of his own.

In his *Aspects of the Novel* (1927) E. M. Forster (1879–1970) divided characters into two types – the 'round', and the 'flat'. He considered that the 'flat' characters were the descendants of the simplified 'types' of earlier drama, who in turn derived from the boastful soldier, angry old men and bashful young lovers of earlier Roman and Italian comedy. Such characters, he believed, are often associated with a repeated catch-phrase, which carries the essential clue to the kind of person he is. The 'round' character is more highly organised; such characters, Forster says, are 'ready for extended life'. They are so well-realised that we can almost imagine them living in the world beyond the book.

This convenient division is perhaps too simple. It is a common-place of criticism that characters in fiction do not live beyond the confines of the art which produced them; yet the 'extended life' of some characters does seem to be demonstrated within the work of art itself. Perhaps the way novelists present character is not unrelated to the perception of personality in everyday life. It is easy to see some people – parents, teachers, policemen, politicians – as stereotypes: we expect them to conform to very narrow criteria of behaviour, and not to vary much beyond them. The terms used to describe them will cluster at one end or the other of a limited set of evaluative words. People whom we know better however will not be seen in this way: they will be described in more diverse and detailed terms. Their behaviour will be too complex to be summoned up in a convenient shorthand.

There seems good sense in distinguishing between 'primary' and 'secondary' characters. The point of view from which a novel is narrated establishes a kind of perspective along which the reader's attention is directed. Even if the novel surveys a wide terrain – be it

War and Peace or *Middlemarch* — only a few characters will be followed with close attention. As we have already seen, some characters exist merely for the light they can throw on others or for the service they can do for them. They are not accorded the full freedom of action which we might think is peculiarly human.

Perhaps the essential difference between types of character is whether they are seen *externally*, as collections of habits and mannerisms, as wearers of particular styles of dress or as utterers of distinctive kinds of sentences, or *internally* as being capable of self-reflection, of doubt, of acts of judgement, of sustained reasoning or deliberate acts of will. Some authors are better than others at conveying a sense of psychological depth, though the success of a novel may not depend upon the writer's ability to do so. Generally speaking, Dickens is not successful when he tries to present characters whose inner lives are complicated by mixed motives or unconventional interests. Although he is good at suggesting lives which are dissatisfied or unfulfilled — think of Edith Dombey, or Miss Wade (in *Little Dorrit*) or Louisa Gradgrind (in *Hard Times*) — he is content to present these states of mind without close analysis. George Eliot is very different: in *Middlemarch* she describes the workings of her characters' minds — their moments of choice, of regret or remorse or indecision — in minute detail. But even in *Middlemarch* the design of her novel distinguishes between the characters who are to be presented fully and those who are treated in a simpler way. Of the four main pairs of couples — whether married or to-be-married — only two are treated in depth: the marriage of Dorothea Brooke, the bright young heroine of the novel, to the dry scholar, Casaubon, is examined closely as is the marriage of the promising young Doctor Lydgate to the rather vacuous provincial beauty, Rosamund Vincy. Even among these four people, George Eliot chooses to show Dorothea and Lydgate in greatest depth, perhaps simply because they are people of talent and potentiality, whose conflicting impulses and instinctive energy make for the greatest interest. In other words, George Eliot endows them with some of the characteristics she most admires as well as some of the defects which are most likely to thwart their best and most effective selves.

Characters of this kind must have the capacity to develop consistently through time. Dickens's magnanimous dustman, Mr Boffin, in *Our Mutual Friend* becomes a miser for a time before beaming out once more in undimmed philanthropic glow, but even his pretence at miserliness is unconvincing: the characters in this novel are used for very different purposes than those of psychological realism. The central characters of Jane Austen or George Eliot or Henry James have the capacity to develop through time. They change according to intelligible schemes, part moral, part psychological, which are made clear (explicitly or implicitly) by the novelists themselves, for each of whom truthfulness has a very high value. In the novels of Joseph Conrad (1857–1924), however, the concept of character itself is much more mysterious, much less open to intellectual analysis. Conrad gives us the sense of the depth of human personality, but he also suggests that it may be unplumbable.

Whatever differences there may be in the methods novelists use to present their characters, it is a mistake to apply to them simply the knowledge of life that we bring to them ourselves. For one thing the novelist may be describing ways of life which are totally beyond our experience. It may require patient attention on our part to grasp the principles by which his characters have been made. It may be, however, that the life of the characters is far more related to their function within the overall structure of the novel and that we should pay particular attention to how the characters are illuminated by patterns of symbolism or imagery in which the life of the novel may be found.

Setting

Much that has been said of character applies to setting. There is nothing accidental about where a novelist chooses to set his novel. Setting, character and action are linked and interrelated. A novelist writes for a readership which he or she has in mind: knowledge, attitudes and interests are implied in what is written. Jane Austen is sometimes blamed for her lack of concern about the Napoleonic wars and the wider political and social events of her day. But the settings of her novels perfectly suit the life she wishes to study. In *Northanger Abbey*, for example, the city of Bath is just the right place for testing the character of a young woman of the class and background of Catherine Morland, just as London might be for a contemporary version of her. Readers of the novel will be aware how little extraneous topographical interest Jane Austen allows herself. Her Bath – Catherine's Bath – is nothing other than the city of fashionable diversion – of balls, assemblies, theatres, and promenades – which it had become in the late eighteenth century. In examining *Tess of the d'Urbervilles* we noticed how closely place, action and theme are connected, so that change of place marks a link in the progressive deterioration of Tess's fortunes. In *The Old Wives' Tale* (1908) by Arnold Bennett (1867–1931), provincial England and Paris are contrasted as places where two young English sisters live out their lives. But one of the points made by the book is that character, and the effect of early upbringing, may be stronger than differences of environment. Sir Walter Scott makes considerable use of the differences between the wild Scottish highlands with their close and fierce clan loyalties and the settled commercial life of the lowlands, between the attachment to old loyalties of the owners of semi-feudal castles and the more shallowly rooted business attitudes of the townsmen. Russian novelists have made us familiar with a difference between the outlook and attitudes of Moscow and St Petersburg, which is cultural, social and moral as well as geographical. Contrasts of place serve as means of structuring the novel just as contrasts of character do.

Setting is often minutely particular: details of geography or topography may be as firmly discriminated as the words a writer chooses for particular effects. Jane Austen's references to Bath can only be understood if we know what Jane Austen assumed her contemporaries would take for granted. The names of streets or districts may have connotations which matter for the interpretation of the novel. Maps – especially historical maps – guidebooks, memoirs and reference books of all kinds can help to make precise the meanings which the novelist has attached to the settings of his novel. This is not to say that the fictional setting bears any resemblance to places recorded in gazetteers: reference books of this kind must be used with care. The connotation of settings depends on context. The London, or Wessex, or Paris of Dickens, or Hardy, or Henry James may be very different from what the historian or geographer has seen of them. Everything which goes into the novel has passed, as Henry James puts it, through the crucible of the novelist's imagination, but sometimes the difference between fact and fiction offers some help in assessing the distinctive qualities of the imaginative selection he has made.

Symbolism and Imagery

Character, action, and setting are all abstract words which refer to the reader's understanding of the writer's text; they are generalisations

which we create from our memory of what we have read. In earlier
fiction it may be possible to isolate extended descriptions of people,
place and action, but in modern novels our knowledge of these things
may be much more indirect. The 'point of view' which the novelist has
chosen will determine a stance from which we are to see the world of
the novel, and this is likely to be highly selective. The novelist may
choose one character as the filter through which the world of the novel
is to be seen, and if the novelist does not wholly identify with his
character, he may look for ways to modify the force which this unified
vision might otherwise have on the reader. Techniques of this kind have
long been familiar in poetry and drama. Poets have written dramatic
monologues in which a character is allowed to communicate his
thoughts directly to the reader; dramatists writing soliloquies which
might be delivered when the character is alone on the stage have done
the same. If such a self-description or self-justification were accepted
uncritically, rogues, villains and tricksters might be taken for honest
men. The writer had so to manage the tone and content of what was
said to suggest to the audience that another view of the character was
possible. What was needed was a method of suggesting the distance
between author and character without some direct intervention by the
author himself.

Other modern novelists have been more interested in expressing a
personal vision of the world which was not confined to examining
psychological motivation or the implications of moral choice. In this
case the novelist had to find a way of shaping his novel, of finding a
means of expressing a personal vision which was not fully expressed by
what his characters said and did. If the novelist now denied himself the
easy luxury of being present in his novel, of explaining what was
happening in it, and of pressing home a coherent set of didactic
conclusions on his reader – and many nineteenth-century English
novelists did this – how could he retain some control over the meaning
of his text?

One answer to both problems lay in extending his use of metaphor.
Metaphor, after all, is the application of terms which are well
understood to circumstances which are not so clear; it is a means
of altering vision, and one aim of the modern novelist was to make his
reader *see*. Individual metaphors may in time be trodden into cliché,
but metaphor does not lose its power to transform ways of seeing. An
object or institution, a person or a group, may be used to represent
something other than itself; by considering something new in the

light of what is already known, our impression of both objects may be changed.

But comparison is not an essential feature of this process which converts object into symbol. In the early chapters of *Bleak House* a detail in the decorative scheme of the house of Mr Tulkinghorn, the rather sinister lawyer in the story, acquires unlooked-for force simply because Dickens makes repeated, though subtly varied, reference to it. It is the figure of a Roman soldier with outstretched pointing arm, painted on the ceiling of Mr Tulkinghorn's room. It is only when the lawyer's body lies dead on the spot to which the soldier seems to be pointing that we see exactly what use Dickens has all along intended to make of this little detail, or motif. In the same novel the Court of Chancery, and its endless, expensive, ineffectual consideration of the disputed will in the case of Jarndyce *v*. Jarndyce, is used metaphorically to stand for the ills of English society. So, too, the weather in the countryside where Sir Leicester and Lady Dedlock live stands for the depression which seems to have settled over part of the English ruling class. But such a metaphor may have many functions: the damp weather of Lincolnshire may also stand for the Dedlocks' loveless marriage.

Novelists may use patterns of repeated motifs, or imagery, to bring their novels under the power of one controlling metaphor which, indirectly but insistently, suggests a way of grasping the novel as a whole. D. H. Lawrence (1885–1930) commonly uses cold and heat to suggest states of deprivation and contentment in his characters. A recurrent motif throughout his fiction is the closed flower which opens to individual maturity and fulfilment. In his most successful novels, such as *The Rainbow* (1915) and *Women in Love* (1920), his characters are seen, as it were, through complex interlacing patterns of vividly visualised episodes, where what is seen is used as an indirect commentary on what the characters do, say and feel. In this way 'images' (words which represent things we can see) become 'imagery', words which are used metaphorically to comment on character or action.

Here is a characteristic example from *The Rainbow*, in which the principal character, Ursula Brangwen, reflects on her life (the 'it' of the first sentence):

Already it was a history. In every phase she was so different. Yet she was always Ursula Brangwen. But what did it mean, Ursula Brangwen? She did not know what she was. Only she was full of

rejection, of refusal. Always, always she was spitting out her mouth
the ash and grit of disillusion, of falsity. She could only stiffen in
rejection. She seemed always negative in her action.

That which she was, positively, was dark and unrevealed, it could
not come forth. It was like a seed buried in dry ash. This world in
which she lived was like a circle lighted by a lamp. This lighted area,
lit up by man's completest consciousness, she thought was all the
world; that here all was disclosed for ever. Yet all the time, within
the darkness she had been aware of points of light, like the eyes of
wild beasts, gleaming, penetrating, vanishing. And her soul had
acknowledged in a great heave of terror only the outer darkness.
This inner circle of light in which she lived and moved, wherein
the trains rushed and the factories ground out their machine-produce
and the plants and the animals worked by the light of science and
knowledge, suddenly it seemed like the area under an arc-lamp,
wherein the mothers and children played in the security of blinding
light, not even knowing there was any darkness, because they stayed
in the light.[6]

Readers of Lawrence must be able to grasp the implications of his
metaphors, and to move nimbly from one metaphor to the next. In
this passage Ursula is considering the mystery of being alive, the
paradoxical sense of continuity within the perpetual change of
individual experience. But Ursula feels that her life is unsatisfactory; it
does not measure up to her idea of what it might be. It is ashes in her
mouth: she is a seed, capable of growth, planted in ashes that stifle
and do not nourish. Her real being is hidden from her. At this point
Lawrence's metaphor changes. Ursula widens her consideration to cover
the whole of her environment, and Lawrence's metaphor changes from
the seed, fallen among ash, to a lamp which lights up a small patch of
ground, but which makes the surrounding darkness appear impenetrable
and threatening.

The most powerful analogy in this passage, however, is one which is
not fully expressed. As Lawrence moves from the simile of the ash to
the simile of the lamp light, the reader is made to compare two kinds of
darkness — on the one hand, the nurturing darkness of the soil, which is
where the seed ought to be; on the other hand, the frightening darkness
beyond the circle of the lamp. Suppose we think of that darkness, too,
as nurturing and sustaining. Suppose we consider that the dark beyond
the lamp-light might be to Ursula's spirit what the darkness of the soil

would be to the seed. In that case our conventional association of 'light' with 'good' and 'dark' with 'danger' would have to be revised.

Observe how Lawrence moves from 'lamp' to 'arc-lamp', which suggests that the light of the lamp falls on a very restricted area. See how he moves from suggesting that light provides safety to the idea that this safety is 'security' — a limited kind of freedom which may be stifling in the end. Notice too how this area of 'security' is linked with moths (and self-destruction) and children (immaturity). To analyse the imagery of this passage is to make crudely explicit what Lawrence expects the reader to grasp immediately. But becoming conscious of how these metaphors work may help the reader to notice other less obvious examples. Consider the following paragraphs which appear in the preceding chapter of Lawrence's novel:

And she gave herself to all that she loved in Cossethay, passionately, because she was going away now. She wandered about to her favourite spots. There was a place where she went trespassing to find the snowdrops that grew wild. It was evening and the winter-darkened meadows were full of mystery. When she came to the woods an oak tree had been newly chopped down in the dell. Pale drops of flowers glimmered many under the hazels, and by the sharp, golden splinters of wood that were splashed about, the grey-green blades of snowdrop leaves pricked unheeding, the drooping still little flowers were without heed.

Ursula picked some lovingly, in an ecstasy. The golden chips of wood shone yellow like sunlight, the snowdrops in the twilight were like first stars of night. And she, alone amongst them was wildly happy to have found her way into such a glimmering dusk, to the intimate little flowers, and the splash of wood chips like sunshine over the twilight of the ground. She sat down on the felled tree and remained awhile remote.

Going home, she left the purplish dark of the trees for the green lane, where the puddles shone long and jewel-like in the rut, the land about her was darkened, and the sky a jewel overhead. Oh, how amazing it was to her! It was almost too much. She wanted to run, and sing, and cry out for very wildness and poignancy, cry out the deep things in her heart, so she was still, and almost sad with loneliness.[7]

There are, of course, metaphors in this passage — the chips of wood 'like sunlight'; the snowdrops 'like stars of night' and so on – but these metaphors play a minor role in the composition of the paragraphs. What we notice here are images – words denoting things which can be seen and touched – snowdrops, woodchips, trees, puddles, woods and sky. Can this visual scene signify more than its surface appearance? Is Ursula's pleasure in it caused by anything more than its visual beauty? Well, Ursula's pleasure turns to sadness because she cannot express 'the deep things in her heart'. What are they, and how are they related to what she sees? What we remark about the images here is that they are related to one another by contrast of light and dark, perhaps too by contrast of life and death. There is no doubt that the woodchips and the snowdrops are *contrasted*: look at the structure of the sentence, 'The golden chips of wood shone yellow like sunlight, the snowdrops in the twilight were like first stars of night.' Each half of it consists of directly contrasted elements: 'golden chips', 'snowdrops'; 'sunlight, 'twilight'; 'shone yellow', 'were like first stars of night'. In the previous paragraph snowdrops and woodchips have simply been set side by side ('by the sharp, golden splinters of wood that were splashed about, the grey-green blades of snowdrops pricked unheeding' – notice that 'by' here means 'alongside'). But even in this sentence there is a metaphor that might go unobserved; what is the effect of the word 'splashed' – does it mean, simply, 'strewn', or does it mean, 'spilled'? Has it to do with the fact that the oak has been chopped down? What is it that the snowdrops do not heed? Could it be the death of the oak? Notice how the word 'blade', perfectly properly applied to the leaf of the snowdrops, picks up connotations of 'knife' and 'sword', as we read the word 'pricked' that follows. And used without a following noun – used intransitively – the verbs 'pricked' suggests that the flowers, in contrast to the oak, are conscious, attentive, tingling, erect, ready to strike.

This reading suggests that death is associated with brightness here, as darkness is with life. As Ursula goes home through the darkened woods, the jewel of the puddle reflects the jewel of the sky; there is something precious to be found here. Notice that Ursula had gone to find just these wild snowdrops. The inclusion of the definite article in 'the snowdrops that grew wild' makes it clear that it was *these* wild snowdrops she went to find – not just some wild snowdrops she happened to find there. She 'trespassed' to find them – went beyond bounds herself. And when she tried to cry out 'the deep things in her heart', it was something of that wildness she wanted to express. But how beautifully Lawrence makes Ursula, in her despair of expressing herself, go 'still' — just like the snowdrops, as they are described in the first paragraph.

By extraordinary verbal skill — how consciously exercised we cannot tell — Lawrence converts his 'images' into 'imagery'. The woodland scene offers some analogy of Ursula herself, dead and yet alive, recognising that this woodland is herself, and yet not quite seeing its significance. In the passage we considered earlier, Lawrence makes his metaphors of darkness and light explicit, but it is very hard to avoid concluding that the same metaphors operate, much less obtrusively, in the passage we have just considered.

Language and Style

Not every reader will agree with the analysis of this last passage. In cases of this kind, meaning is potential; interpretation may be forced to press beyond what the language of the novel says. This is the language of implication, not of statement. There is room for divergent interpretations though each is constrained by what the English language itself is able to bear. A sensitive responsiveness to the language of the novel is the most significant skill which a reader of literature must acquire. It is also the most fundamental material out of which the broader categories discussed in this chapter are created. Plot, action, character and setting are constructs — frameworks — too rigid, sometimes — fashioned from the words the writer arranges on his pages. In reading a novel we must be able to take account of the broad plans and strategies of the writer, but we only know of their existence by our response to the details of his text. Just as each author has a characteristic handwriting, so he uses language in a personally distinctive way. How he writes a sentence holds a clue to how he sees the world.

To look back over more than two centuries of novel-writing in English is to see many changes in the ways people have lived and in their assumptions about the limits of human behaviour; it is to see many changes in the form of the novel; it is also to see many changes in the form of the English language. One of the chapters of James Joyce's *Ulysses,* describing the events of the birth of a baby boy, is written in a parody of the history of English literary language from Anglo-Saxon to the experimental English of Joyce himself. More recently, Russell

Hoban (1925–   ) has written a novel, *Riddley Walker* (1980), in the language he imagines English might be in a post-nuclear Britain, which has lost all its heritage except what inheres in the language itself. An introduction to the novel must in the end be an introduction to the language of the novel, to the customs, habits, attitudes and beliefs which are caught in the web of that language, and to the wider world of buildings, objects and artefacts, cities and streets, to whose significance it holds the key.

References

Chapter 1
1. Jane Austen, *Northanger Abbey* (Harmondsworth: Penguin Books, 1972) pp. 57–8.
2. James Joyce, *Finnegans Wake* (London: Faber, 1972), p. 281.

Chapter 2
1. C. T. Onions (ed.), *Sweet's Anglo-Saxon Reader in Prose and Verse*, 12th edn (London: Oxford University Press, 1950) p. 29 [Author's translation].
2. Walter W. Skeat (ed.), *Specimens of English Literature*, 3rd edn (London: Oxford University Press, 1880) pp. 160–1 [Author's translation].
3. Miguel de Cervantes Saavedra, *The Adventures of Don Quixote*, translated by J. M. Cohen (Harmondsworth: Penguin Books, 1950) p. 624.
4. *Fables of Aesop* [Author's translation].
5. John Bunyan, *The Pilgrim's Progress* (London, Edinburgh and New York: Thomas Nelson and Sons, 1902) pp. 46–7.
6. Ibid., pp. 127–8.
7. J. M. Edmonds (ed.), *The Characters of Theophrastus* (London: Loeb Classical Library, 1929) pp. 47–8.
8. Charles Dickens, *Little Dorrit* (Harmondsworth: Penguin Books, 1967) pp. 192–3.
9. John Earle: 'A Child' in *Character Writings in the Seventeenth Century*, ed. John Morley (London: Routledge, 1891) p. 189.
10. Sheldon Sachs, *Fiction and the Shape of Belief* (Chicago and London: The University of Chicago Press, 1964) p. 27.

Chapter 3
1. Richard Graves, *The Spiritual Quixote* (London: Peter Davies, 1926) pp. 73–4.
2. Ibid., p. 75.
3. Ibid., pp. 75–6.
4. Emily Brontë, *Wuthering Heights* (Harmondsworth: Penguin Books, 1965) pp. 66–7.
5. Charles Dickens, *Great Expectations* (Harmondsworth: Penguin

Books, 1965) pp. 37—8.
6. Ibid., pp. 38—9.
7. Thomas Hardy, *Tess of the d'Urbervilles* (London: Macmillan and Co., 1950) pp. 34—6.
8. Christina Stead, *For Love Alone* (London: Peter Davies, 1945) p. 189.
9. Samuel Selvon, *The Lonely Londoners* (London: Longman Caribbean, 1972) pp. 57—8.
10. Ayi Kwei Armah, *The Beautyful Ones are not yet Born* (London: Heinemann, 1969) pp. 34—5.
11. Ibid., pp. 117—18.

Chapter 4
1. James Joyce, *Ulysses* (London: The Bodley Head, 1960) p. 65.
2. Henry James, *The Wings of the Dove* (London: Eyre & Spottiswoode, 1969) p. 11.
3. Jane Austen, *Mansfield Park* (London: Oxford University Press, 1934) pp. 388—9.
4. Dickens, *Great Expectations*, p. 46.
5. Ibid., p. 48.
6. Henry Fielding, *Tom Jones* (Harmondsworth: Penguin Books, 1966) pp. 495—6.
7. Sir Walter Scott, *Old Mortality* (Harmondsworth: Penguin Books, 1975) p. 208.
8. Ibid., p. 209.
9. William Thackeray, *Pendennis* (Harmondsworth: Penguin Books, 1972) pp. 189—90.

Chapter 5
1. Graham Greene, *The End of the Affair* (Harmondsworth: Penguin Books, 1975) p. 7.
2. Jane Austen, *Pride and Prejudice* (Harmondsworth: Penguin Books, 1972) p. 163.
3. Ibid., pp. 165—6.
4. Ibid., p. 168.
5. Ibid., p. 166.
6. Ibid., pp. 69—70.
7. Ibid., pp. 234—5.
8. Ibid., pp. 236—7.
9. Ibid., pp. 369—70.
10. Ibid., pp. 101—2.
11. Ibid., p. 102.
12. Ibid., p. 73.
13. Ibid., pp. 102—3.
14. Ibid., pp. 135—6.
15. F. Scott Fitzgerald, *The Great Gatsby* (Harmondsworth: Penguin Books, 1950) pp. 7—8.
16. Ibid., pp. 105—6.
17. Ibid., p. 105.

Chapter 7

1. Hardy, *Tess of the d'Urbervilles*, pp. 49–50.
2. Ibid., pp. 10–11.
3. Ibid., p. 135.
4. Ibid., p. 138.
5. Ibid., pp. 365–6.
6. Ibid., pp. 360–1.
7. Ibid., p. 359.
8. Ibid., p. 34.
9. Ibid., pp. 35–6.
10. Ibid., p. 24.
11. Ibid., pp. 78–9.
12. Ibid., pp. 81–2.
13. Ibid., pp. 85–6.
14. Ibid., p. 252.
15. Ibid., pp. 159–60.
16. Alfred Lord Tennyson: 'Maud' in Christopher Ricks, *The Poems of Tennyson* (London: Longman, 1969) p. 1077.
17. Hardy, *Tess of the d'Urbervilles*, pp. 169–70.
18. Ibid., pp. 230–1.
19. Ibid., p. 294.
20. Ibid., pp. 273–4.
21. Ibid., p. 276.
22. Ibid., p. 253.
23. Ibid., p. 274.
24. 1 Corinthians 13, 4–7.
25. Hardy, *Tess of the d'Urbervilles*, pp. 310–11.

Chapter 8

1. R. K. Narayan, *The English Teacher* (Chicago and London: The University of Chicago Press, 1980) p. 19.
2. Ibid., p. 19.
3. Chinua Achebe, *Things Fall Apart* (London: Heinemann, 1967) p. 155.
4. Ibid., p. 62.
5. Ibid., p. 187.
6. Ibid., p. 160.

Chapter 9

1. Nathaniel Hawthorne, Preface to *The House of the Seven Gables* quoted in Miriam Allott, *Novelists on the Novel* (London: Routledge, 1965) p. 51.
2. Charles Dickens, *Hard Times* (Harmondsworth: Penguin Books, 1969) p. 58.
3. Wilkie Collins, *The Woman in White* (Harmondsworth: Penguin Books, 1974) p. 58.
4. Ibid., p. 76.
5. Charles Dickens, *Our Mutual Friend* (Harmondsworth: Penguin

Books, 1971) pp. 178–9.
6. D. H. Lawrence, *The Rainbow* (Harmondsworth: Penguin Books, 1970) p. 437.
7. Ibid., p. 420.

Bibliography

Abrams, M. H., *A Glossary of Literary Terms*, fourth edition (New York: Holt, Rinehart, 1981).

Allott, Mirian, *Novelists on the Novel* (London: Routledge, 1965).

Booth, Wayne C., *The Rhetoric of Fiction* (Chicago: University of Chicago Press, 1961).

Bradbury, M., *The Novel Today* (London: Fontana/Collins, 1977).

Forster, E. M., *Aspects of the Novel* (Harmondsworth: Penguin Books, 1976).

Halperin, John (ed.), *The Theory of the Novel* (New York: Oxford University Press, 1974).

Hewitt, Douglas, *The Approach to Fiction* (London: Longman, 1972).

Lodge, David, *The Language of Fiction* (London: Routledge, 1966).

Lodge, David, *The Modes of Modern Writing* (London: Edward Arnold, 1977).

Lubbock, Percy, *The Craft of Fiction* (London: Jonathan Cape, 1921).

Murdoch, Iris, *The Sovereignty of Good* (London: Routledge, 1970).

Raban, Jonathan, *The Technique of Modern Fiction* (London: Edward Arnold, 1968).

Scholes, Robert and Kellogg, Robert, *The Nature of Narrative* (London: Oxford University Press, 1966).

Stevick, Philip (ed.), *The Theory of the Novel* (New York: The Free Press, 1967).

Index

Subjects